CHARTS *on* Open Theism *and* Orthodoxy

CHARTS *on* Open Theism *and* Orthodoxy

H. Wayne House *with* Matt Power

Charts on Open Theism and Orthodoxy

Published by Kregel Publications, a division of Kregel, Inc., P.O. Box 2607, Grand Rapids, MI 49501.

ISBN 0-8254-2880-7

Printed in the United States of America

03 04 05 06 07 / 5 4 3 2 1

To
Norm Geisler,
a friend of many years,
and a staunch defender
of the orthodox faith.

Contents

4. Historical Understandings of Ultimate Reality and God

5. Historical Views on the Attributes of God

Preface

This is a far different book from any of my other works. In *Charts on Open Theism and Orthodoxy* I offer no analysis and seek to make no judgment of Open Theism (also referred to as the Open View of God, Neotheism, or Openness Theology). For those who have read the book I co-authored with Norman L. Geisler, they are very aware that I consider Open Theism—which is making inroads within evangelicalism—as being a serious deviation from historic Christianity and from a proper interpretation of the Bible. The purpose of this work is to expose readers to Open Theism and enable them to thoroughly compare it with historic Christian views, such as Arminianism and Calvinism, as well as Process Theism—a clear false teaching, even in the thought of Open Theists. Openness theologians often seek to present themselves as being merely a variation of Arminianism, while those who oppose them believe them to be closer, at many junctures, to Process Theism. The reader can decide.

A few words about technical matters are in order. First, though there was an attempt to find quotes from all representative groups for every category, at times only three positions may be represented. Second, there is no personal comment within the various column cells; all are quotes. The quotes, however, do not have quotation marks. Third, by necessity I have had to be selective in the quotations for the various views presented herein, and there may be disagreement as to whether the quotes chosen best represent the respective positions, but I have attempted to be fair.

Hopefully this book will enhance and help clarify the current debate within evangelicalism on the Open View of God versus the historic Christian faith.

Acknowledgments

I wish to express my thanks to Matt Power for all of his help in the production of this book, and to Dennis Hillman, publisher with Kregel Publications, for his patience and encouragement. Additional thanks to the Kregel editorial and production team—Steve Barclift, Sarah De Mey, Moriah Sharp, and Rachel Warren—for their professionalism and extra patience.

The author gratefully acknowledges permission to quote from the following works:

Gregory A. Boyd, *God at War*. © 1997 by Gregory A. Boyd. Published by InterVarsity Press. Used by permission.

Gregory A. Boyd, *God of the Possible*. © 2000 Baker Book House. Used by permission.

Gregory A. Boyd, *Satan and the Problem of Evil*. © 2001 by Gregory A. Boyd. Published by InterVarsity Press. Used by permission.

Clark Pinncock, *Most Moved Mover: A Theology of God's Openness*. © 2001 Paternoster Press. Used by permission.

Clark H. Pinnock, Richard Rice, John Sanders, William Hasker, and David Basinger, *The Openness of God*. ©1994 InterVarsity Press. Used by permission.

John Ernest Sanders, *The God Who Risks*. © 1998 by John Ernest Sanders. Published by InterVarsity Press. Used by permission.

PART ONE
Terms and Definitions

Terms and Definitions

	Orthodoxy	Open Theism
Simplicity	When we speak of the simplicity of God, we use the term to describe the state or quality of being simple, the condition of being free from division into parts, and therefore from compositeness. It means that God is not composite and is not susceptible of division in any sense of the word. . . . The simplicity of God follows from some of His other perfections; from His Self-existence, which excludes the idea that some thing preceded Him, as in the case of compounds; and from His immutability, which could not be predicated of His nature, if it were made up of parts. Berkhof, *Systematic Theology,* 62. God's whole being, inclusive of all attributes, is present in each of the discrete attributes that faith recognizes and celebrates. God is fully and simultaneously all these attributes. . . . This notion is interwoven with faith's affirmation of God's simplicity. God is not divided up into our petty conceptions of God's attributes. In all attributes, God is, and remains, simply and completely God. Oden, *The Living God,* 40. See also Henry, *God, Revelation and Authority,* 1:131.	. . . The whole doctrine of Divine simplicity arises from a misinterpretation of the truth that God is not divisible into parts, that all his properties are interconnected. God's properties are necessarily connected in a reciprocally determining whole, and are not just contingently or fortuitously related. . . . However, I can see no a priori reason why the Divine being should not be internally complex, each part depending essentially upon the unity of the whole. Thus one is not compelled to take the step to a wholly ineffable being, so simple that our complex analytic concepts could not grasp it at all. Ward, *Rational Theology and the Creativity of God,* 64. Let us not treat the attributes of God independently of the Bible but view the biblical metaphors as reality-depicting descriptions of the living God, whose very being is self-giving love. When we do so, God's unity will not be viewed as a mathematical oneness but as a unity that includes diversity. . . . Pinnock, *Most Moved Mover,* 27.
Pure Actuality	*Actuality* or *act* is the opposite of potentiality. Through various causes, a being that is, say, potentially a tree, becomes one actually. . . . (God, of course, is "in act" in every respect.) . . . Having no passive potentiality, God is "pure act," the "pure act of being." Frame, *The Doctrine of God,* 223. The citation of a few definitions [of God] may be useful. "The first ground of all being; the divine spirit which, unmoved itself, moves all; absolute, efficient principle; absolute notion; absolute end."—*Aristotle*. This definition conforms somewhat to the author's four forms of cause. It contains more truth of a definition than some given by professedly Christian philosophers. Miley, *Systematic Theology*, 1:59.	Pure actuality means . . . God cannot have real relationships with a changeable world because that would involve give and take. Pinnock, *Most Moved Mover,* 117. . . . From Plato, Aristotle and the subsequent Hellenistic tradition, the church arrived at the notion that God was altogether unmoved . . . and purely actual. Yet it was precisely these features of the church's doctrine of God that logically undermined the integrity of the [spiritual] warfare worldview [held by the early church Fathers]. Boyd, *God at War,* 67.
Necessity	God . . . has the ground of His existence in Himself. . . . God is the uncaused, who exists by the necessity of His own being, and therefore necessarily . . . [God] is conceived of as the self-existent and as the ultimate ground of all things. . . . Berkhof, *Systematic Theology,* 58.	. . . It is, I think, easy enough to show fairly conclusively that "God exists" is not logically necessary. . . . For the theist the existence of God is a tremendous thing, the most fundamental truth about the universe. It seems to trivialize it to say that it holds for the same reason as does the truth that all bachelors are unmarried. Swinburne, *The Coherence of Theism,* 265.

Terms and Definitions

	Orthodoxy	Open Theism
Necessity	. . . I agree with Aquinas's view that God exists necessarily. He does not merely happen to exist; he must exist. . . . His nonexistence is metaphysically impossible in that nothing or nobody can prevent him from existing or put him out of existence. Frame, *The Doctrine of God,* 230–31. We have the idea of the most perfect Being, a Being than whom a greater or more perfect cannot be conceived. This idea includes, and must include, actual existence, because actual existence is of the necessary content of the idea of the most perfect. . . . Hence we must admit the actual [and necessary] existence, for only with this content can we have the idea of the most perfect Being. [Summarizing Anselm's ontological argument.] Miley, *Systematic Theology*, 1:74.	I do not mean that God is subject to change involuntarily, which would make God a contingent being. . . . Pinnock, *The Openness of God,* 118. To say that "God exists" is logically necessary is not to trivialize the concept of God by making his existence a matter of verbal definition. "God exists" is not made true by any arbitrary set of axioms. It is made true by the existence of God, and what makes it non-contingent is that there is no possible world in which God does not exist. I conclude that the notion of a logically necessary being is a coherent one, and if this could be demonstrated, it would follow that any such being would exist. Ward, *Rational Theology and the Creativity of God,* 44. [God] is not wholly immutable and necessary, for he is also changing and contingent. Ward, *Rational Theology and the Creativity of God,* 159.
Aseity	The Self-existence of God *(aseitas)* denotes that the ground of his being is in himself. . . . God is the uncaused Being, and in this respect differs from all other beings. Shedd, *Dogmatic Theology,* 338. I am unable to verify [Bavinck's] distinction between aseity and independence. . . . [A]seity . . . refers to God "as he is in himself," apart from creation, while independence presupposes a created world (at least in God's plan) from which he is independent. On that account, aseity is more fundamental. God is independent of the world because in himself he is *a se*. And, contrary to Bavinck, I don't think that aseity need be limited to existence; like independence, it can be freely applied to everything God is and does, to his attributes, decrees, and works. For practical purposes, then, I would consider the two terms interchangeable, noting that aseity takes the concept to a deeper level. Frame, *The Doctrine of God,* 601. To affirm that God is independent or necessary means that God depends on no cause external to God. God's life is contingent upon nothing else. This is sometimes called aseity . . . or self-existence, or underived existence. To say that God is . . . self-existent (or self-subsistent) means simply that God is without origin, that God is the only ground of God's being, and that there is no cause prior to God. . . . This supreme being has not at some point in time *become* the Supreme Being, but simply *is,* and has never been otherwise. Oden, *The Living God,* 55.	Since it sees God as dependent on the world in certain respects, the open view of God differs from much conventional theology. Yet we believe that this dependence does not detract from God's greatness, it only enhances it. Rice, "Biblical Support for a New Perspective"; in Pinnock, *The Openness of God,* 16. Our account of [aseity] will depend crucially on what kind of being we suppose God to be. . . . I conclude that it is not logically possible that any agent could bring about God's existence if God is necessarily an eternal being. Swinburne, *The Coherence of Theism,* 256. Another troubling aspect of the teaching advocated by Augustine and Piper is, Why God does not intend to save all? If God must express his justice in the damnation of certain people, then God is *dependent* on the damned (as well as the saved) for the fulfillment of his nature. It would seem that God *needs* the damned in order to be who God wants to be. This would appear to call into question God's self-sufficiency *(aseity),* that God was free to create or not create, and sounds in certain respects like panentheism, wherein God needs the world in order to be God. Sanders, *The God Who Risks,* 242.

Terms and Definitions

	Orthodoxy	Open Theism
Immutability	Immutability is an incommunicable attribute of God by which is denied of him not only all change, but also all possibility of change, as much with respect to existence as to will. Turretin, *Institutes of Elenctic Theology,* 1.3.11.1. Creation did not produce a change in God, but in creatures. . . . When God became the Creator, he was not changed in himself (for nothing new happened to him, for from eternity he had the efficacious will of creating the world in time) . . . Turretin, *Institutes of Elenctic Theology*, 1.3.11.5. God's aseity implies his immutability. Now at first it may seem that this immutability is unsupported by Scripture. The Bible everywhere represents God as being in very close contact with the world. In the beginning he created heaven and earth; hence, from the state of non-creative activity he proceeded to that of creative activity. . . . Similarly, the people of God experience at one time God's wrath, then again his love. . . . Notwithstanding all this, Scripture testifies that in all these various relations and experiences God remains ever the same. Though everything perishes, he endures; he remains what he is. . . . He is Jehovah, who remaineth eternally the same . . . being immutable in his existence and essence, he is also unchangeable in his thoughts and will, in all his purposes and decrees: he is not a man that he should repent. Bavinck, *The Doctrine of God,* 145–46. We previously pointed out the truth of immutability in the essential being of God. It is the truth of his eternal absolute identity of being. He is immutable in the plenitude and perfection of his personal attributes. His omniscience, holiness, justice, love, considered simply as attributes, are forever the same. Definite and varying acts of personal agency, and new facts of consciousness . . . are entirely consistent with such immutability. Miley, *Systematic Theology*, 1:221.	God is immutable in essence and in his trustworthiness over time, but in other respects God changes. Pinnock, *The Openness of God,* 117. . . . Scripture depicts God as having a perfect, immutable character but as expressing this character through his wonderfully flexible interactions with his creations. Boyd, *Satan and the Problem of the Evil,* 142. . . . Everything about God must be changeless for the traditional view, whereas the open view sees God as both changeless and changeable. Rice, "Biblical Support for a New Perspective"; in Pinnock, *The Openness of God,* 48. When I say that God is subject to change, I am referring to a uniquely divine kind of changeability. I do not mean that God is subject to change involuntarily, which would make God a contingent being, but that God allows the world to touch him, while being transcendent over it. Pinnock, *The Openness of God,* 118. We must let Scripture speak to our definitions of the attributes of God. The Bible's representation of God's changeable faithfulness speaks to the issue of immutability. Pinnock, *Most Moved Mover,* 64. The faithfulness of God has customarily been discussed as a category of divine immutability. This would not be so bad if the personal aspects of God's relationship to us had been kept in mind. Too often, however, immutability has been defined apart from what we know of God in history and has been seen to imply that God is absolutely unchangeable in every respect. Sanders, *The God Who Risks,* 186. As God is primarily a creative intellect, he can create new possibilities or develop and modify old ones. Thus there is no total sum of eternal ideas, but a constantly changing stock of imaginatively created ideas, limited only by God's character as wise, good and loving. This means admitting the strange-sounding axiom that new possibilities can come into being. But if one is clear that possibles only exist in so far as they are conceived by the Divine mind, then it causes no difficulty that God should come to conceive new things—as long as he can change. Ward, *Rational Theology and the Creativity of God,* 154.

Terms and Definitions

	Orthodoxy	Open Theism
Immutability	The biblical witness views God not as immobile or static, but as consistent with his own nature, congruent with the depths of his own personal being, stable. . . . Immutability is sometimes stated in wooden, Aristotelian terms that wholly lack these vital energies of the biblical witness to God's constancy. . . . The divine immutability of purpose and essence does not mean that God is unresponsive or incapable of interaction, but that . . . God's unfailing holy love—is sure and unchanging. Oden, *The Living God,* 112–13.	I believe the route for the Christian philosopher to follow is happily to admit that there are senses in which God does indeed change, i.e. alter. I am quite prepared to say, for example, that he changes in his knowledge of propositions like Davis's hair is now brown, it is now 7 June, 1982, and the like. If anyone wants to insist that this undermines God's immutability I will admit that God is not immutable. . . . Davis, *Logic and the Nature of God,* 47.
Impassibility	Repentance is attributed to God after the manner of men *(anthropopathos)* but must be understood after the manner of God *(theoprepos):* not with respect to his counsel, but to the event; not in reference to his will, but to the thing willed; not to affection and internal grief, but to the effect and external work because he does what a penitent man usually does. Turretin, *Institutes of Elenctic Theology,* 1.3.11.11. And is the Creator and Preserver of the world unconcerned for what he sees therein? . . . Does he sit at ease in the heaven, without regarding the poor inhabitants of earth? It cannot be. . . . He is concerned every moment for what befalls every creature upon earth; and more especially for everything that befalls any of the children of men. Wesley, *The Works of John Wesley,* VI.LXVII:317. That [God] regards the same person now with reprehensive displeasure, and again with approving love, is not only consistent with his immutability, but a requirement of it in view of the moral change in the object of his changed regards. Miley, *Systematic Theology,* 1:221.	The idea of a suffering God is the antithesis of traditional divine attributes such as immutability and impassibility. It contradicts the notion that God is immune to transition, to anything resembling the vicissitudes of human experience. Rice, "Biblical Support for a New Perspective"; in Pinnock, *The Openness of God,* 46. Impassibility . . . suggests that God does not experience sorrow, sadness or pain. It appears to deny that God is touched by the feelings of our infirmities, despite what the Bible eloquently says about his love and his sorrow. Pinnock, *The Openness of God,* 118. The sufferings of God and the cross of Christ speak to the issue of impassibility. Pinnock, *Most Moved Mover,* 64. It is astonishing, when you think about it, that impassibility could have become orthodox belief in the early centuries. Here perhaps more than anywhere else we find the bankruptcy of conventional theology. Divine suffering lies at the heart of the Christian faith. Pinnock, *Most Moved Mover,* 89. [On the classical view of impassibility] God must . . . be apathetic, unaffected by our joys or sorrows. Pinnock, *Most Moved Mover,* 117. . . . The Lord is frequently grieved, frustrated and even amazed at how stiff-necked people are toward him. . . . Boyd, *Satan and the Problem of Evil,* 83.

Terms and Definitions

	Orthodoxy	Open Theism
Eternality	The infinitude of God . . . relatively to duration . . . is his eternity. . . . He is exalted above all the limitations of time. . . . With Him there is no distinction between the present, past, and future; but all things are equally and always present to Him. With Him duration is an eternal now. Hodge, *Systematic Theology,* 1.5.6. All time, or rather all eternity . . . [is] present to him at once, he does not know one thing before another, or one thing after another; but sees all things in one point of view from everlasting to everlasting. As all time, with everything that exists therein, is present with him at once, so he sees at once, whatever was, is, or will be, to the end of time. Wesley, *The Works of John Wesley,* VI.LVIII: 226-27. The almighty, all-wise God sees and knows, from everlasting to everlasting, all that is, that was, and that is to come, through one eternal *now*. With him nothing is either past or future, but all things equally present. He has, therefore, if we speak according to the truth of things, no foreknowledge, no afterknowledge. Wesley, *The Works of John Wesley,* VI.LVIII:230. In its simplest sense, the eternity of God is his existence without beginning or end; in its deepest meaning, his endless existence in absolute unchangeableness of essence or attribute. . . . The question arises . . . whether [God] exists in duration or in an eternal now. There is no eternal now. The terms are contradictory. The notion of duration is inseparable from the notion of being. . . . Being must exist in duration. God is the reality of being, and none the less so because of his personality. Miley, *Systematic Theology,* 1:214–15. There was a time, if "time" it could be called, when God, in the unity of His nature (though subsisting equally in three Divine Persons), dwelt all alone. . . . There was nothing, no one, but God; and that, not for a day, a year, or an age, but "from everlasting." During a past eternity, God was alone: self-contained, self-sufficient, self-satisfied. . . . Pink, *The Attributes of God,* 1–2.	In my view, the Bible depicts God as experiencing duration rather than timelessness or simultaneity. . . . God is everlasting through time rather than timeless or having simultaneity (all of time at once). Sanders, *The God Who Risks,* 319 n. 78. When I say that God is eternal, I mean that God transcends our experience of time, is immune from the ravages of time, is free from our inability to remember, and so forth. Pinnock, *The Openness of God,* 120. . . . the classical-philosophical conception of God as necessarily possessing the traditional Hellenistic attributes of changelessness, timelessness, unrelatedness and so on are no longer regarded as self-evident. . . . The more these attributes are questioned, the more theologians are moving toward an understanding of God and his relationship to the world that can include the sort of contingency, openness and risk that is essential to a genuine warfare perspective of the world. Boyd, *Satan and the Problem of Evil,* 68–69. . . . I am convinced that the Neoplatonic-Augustinian metaphysics is intimately involved in the doctrine of divine timelessness, which cannot and probably should not survive without it. . . . I will venture the prediction that over the long haul the doctrine and the metaphysic will stand or fall together—that the theory of timelessness, if its metaphysical tap root is severed, will eventually shrivel and die. Hasker, *God, Time, and Knowledge,* 183. For me, however, the most difficult aspect of the doctrine [of divine timelessness] to accept is . . . "the problem of the presence of time in eternity." It seems inescapable . . . that if God is eternal, he knows us only by contemplating in eternity his own unchangeable "similitudes," "images," or representations of us. But I find this extremely difficult to accept as the truth of the matter . . . that God in very truth knows us, and relates to us, only as the eternal representations in his own essence—this is a hard doctrine. . . . [To accept divine timelessness] leaves too great a distance between the God who is affirmed theologically and the God who is known through Scripture and experience. Hasker, *God, Time, and Knowledge,* 184.

Terms and Definitions

	Orthodoxy	Open Theism
Transcendence	. . . The world is not God nor any part of God, but something absolutely distinct from God. . . . The universe is not the existence-form of God . . . and God is not simply the life, or soul, or inner law of the world, but enjoys His own eternally complete life above the world, in absolute independence of it. He is the transcendent God. . . . Berkhof, *Systematic Theology,* 134. FROM THE VERY FIRST the Bible designates God as the transcendent ground of the universe. Henry, *God, Revelation and Authority*, V.1:43. While a material ground can answer for the properties of body, only a spiritual ground can answer for the faculties of mind. The divine attributes must have their ground in spiritual being. Miley, *Systematic Theology,* 1:162.	Transcendence refers to [God's] difference or separation from [the world]. The God of deism is wholly transcendent, and the God of pantheism is wholly immanent. Each view emphasizes one attribute to the exclusion of the other. The Christian view of God is different because it attributes both qualities to God. God indeed transcends the world. He is unlike anything he has made and infinitely superior to anything finite. Rice, *The Reign of God,* 77–78. It is important to recognize that God (according to the Bible) is . . . transcendent (that is, self-sufficient, the Creator of the world, ontologically other than creation, sovereign and eternal). . . . Pinnock, *The Openness of God,* 105. . . . God allows the world to touch him, while being transcendent over it. Pinnock, *The Openness of God,* 118.
Immanence	An infinite spirit does not forbid the assumption of the existence of matter. . . . [God] is present in all portions of space. Hodge, *Systematic Theology,* 1.5.5.A. The Bible's central role for miracle, [modernists] said, requires a prescientific worldview that breaches the all-pervading causal continuity demanded by modern scientism. But if, as modernism believed, God is immanent in and revealed in the universal human cultural development, then why did the modernist consider himself as standing in a somewhat transcendent relation to culture? Henry, *God, Revelation and Authority,* V.1:398. . . . it is nothing strange that He who is omnipresent, who "filleth heaven and earth," who is in every place, should see what is in every place, where he is intimately present . . . especially considering, that nothing is distant from Him in whom we all "live, and move, and have our being." Wesley, *The Works of John Wesley,* VI.LXVII:315.	. . . God (according to the Bible) is . . . immanent (that is, present to the world, active within history, involved, relational and temporal). Pinnock, *The Openness of God,* 105. God is on the inside of creation, in the processes not in the gaps. God is immanent throughout the universe in all of its changeableness and contingency and active in the whole long process of its development. The Creator has a mysterious relationship with every bit of matter and with every person. Pinnock, *The Openness of God,* 112–13. Immanence refers to God's participation or involvement in the world. . . . [God] is actively involved in the world, momentarily sustaining its operation and guiding it toward the fulfillment of his purposes for it. Rice, *The Reign of God,* 77–78.

Terms and Definitions

	Orthodoxy	Open Theism
Infinity	The infinity of God follows his simplicity and is equally diffused through the other attributes of God, and by it the divine nature is conceived as free from all limit in imperfection. . . . Turretin, *Institutes of Elenctic Theology,* 1.3.8.1. God is said to be infinite in essence in three ways: (1) originally, because he is absolutely independent . . . (2) formally, because he has an absolutely infinite *(apeiron)* essence; (3) virtually, because his activity has no finite sphere. . . . Turretin, *Institutes of Elenctic Theology,* 1.3.8.8. The Infinity of God is the divine essence viewed as having no bounds, or limits. And since limitation implies imperfection, the infinity of God implies that he is perfect in every respect in which he is infinite. Shedd, *Dogmatic Theology,* 1:339.	All this is to say that the assertion "God is infinite" (totally unlike us) is not a meaningful assertion and that arguments based on it should be viewed skeptically. Sanders, *The God Who Risks,* 34. . . . Because God possesses infinite intelligence, his knowledge of might-counterfactuals leaves him no less prepared for the future than his knowledge of determinate aspects of creation. . . . Because he is infinitely intelligent, he does not need to "thin out" his attention over numerous possibilities as we do. . . . He is infinitely attentive to each and every [possibility]. Boyd, *Satan and the Problem of Evil,* 128–29.
Omnipotence	The Divine power is Omnipotence. . . . The Divine power is not to be measured merely by what God has actually effected. Omnipotence is manifested in the works of the actual creation, but it is not exhausted by them. . . . The Divine power is limited only by the absurd and self-contradictory. God can do anything that does not imply a logical impossibility. Shedd, *Dogmatic Theology,* 1:359. It is by removing all the limitations of power, as it exists in us, that we rise to the idea of the omnipotence of God. . . . This simple idea of the omnipotence of God, that He can do without effort, and by a volition, whatever He wills, is the highest conceivable idea of power, and is that which is clearly presented in the Scriptures. Hodge, *Systematic Theology,* 1.5.10.B. . . . God's omnipotence consists in this, that he can do whatever he wants to do. . . . But God cannot will everything. He cannot deny himself. Bavinck, *The Doctrine of God,* 244. . . . It is *impossible* to give a logical explanation of the existence of the world apart from belief in an omnipotent God. . . . God's omnipotence infinitely transcends the unlimited power which is revealed in the universe. Bavinck, *The Doctrine of God,* 245.	God's power is the power of love and a power that gives us life and sustains us. It is not an omnicausality that excludes the autonomy of creatures. God governs with power but also with respect for the God-given freedom of creatures. Despite having the power to control everything, God voluntarily limits the exercise of that power. Pinnock, *Most Moved Mover,* 95. We must not define omnipotence as the power to determine everything but rather as the power that enables God to deal with any situation that arises. Pinnock, *The Openness of God,* 114. Almightiness should . . . be understood under the category of the divine project God has undertaken and not as a formal power. The powerful God *('el shaddai)* of the Bible is the one who is mighty to deliver and to care for his people. . . . God's relationship with us in history is the proper basis for understanding almightiness. Sanders, *The God Who Risks,* 188. Language about omnipotence . . . must be critiqued in light of the sort of omnipotence God has actually exercised in relation to us. . . . The cross and resurrection of Jesus—typifying the way of God in the world—should lead us to smash our idols of the "absolute" placed above the God of salvation history. Sanders, *The God Who Risks,* 188.

Terms and Definitions

	Orthodoxy	Open Theism
Omniscience	God is said to know Himself and all things out of Himself. . . . God knows Himself by the necessity of his nature. . . . Being the cause of all things, God knows everything by knowing Himself; all things possible, by the knowledge of his power, and all things actual, by the knowledge of his own purposes. Hodge, *Systematic Theology*, 1.5.8.B. . . . God's knowledge is, in the first place, all-comprehensive; nothing is outside of the sphere of his omniscience; there is nothing that is not manifest in his sight; all things are naked and laid open before the eyes of him with whom we have to do. This truth has been admitted by all Christian theologians, Jerome excepted. Bavinck, *The Doctrine of God,* 188. God, therefore, understands himself. He knows all things possible, whether they be in the capability of God or of the creature; in active or passive capability; in the capability of operation, imagination, or enunciation. He knows all things that could have an existence, on laying down any hypothesis. He knows other things than himself, those which are necessary and contingent, good and bad, universal and particular, future, present and past, excellent and vile. He knows things substantial and accidental of every kind; the actions and passions, the modes and circumstances of all things; external words and deeds, internal thoughts, deliberations, counsels, and determinations, and the entities of reason, whether complex or simple. All these things, being jointly attributed to the understanding of God, seem to conduce to the conclusion, that God may deservedly be said to know things infinite. Arminius, *Public Disputations,* IV.XXXI. . . . God sees and knows all the properties of the beings that he hath made. He knows all the connexions, dependencies, and relations, and all the ways wherein one of them can affect another. In particular, he sees all the inanimate parts of the creation, whether in heaven above, or in the earth beneath. . . . All these lie naked and open to the eye of the Creator and Preserver of the universe. Wesley, *The Works of John Wesley,* VI.LXVII:316.	[The openness] understanding of omniscience has the advantage of being able to explain in a straightforward fashion both the texts that depict God as knowing the future and those that portray God as not knowing the future in a definite manner. . . . In the openness model of omniscience . . . both sorts of texts are valid and reveal aspects of God's relationship with us. Sanders, *The God Who Risks*, 132. Christian philosophers disagree about the nature of omniscience. . . . Whereas some maintain exhaustive foreknowledge (or omniprescience), others contend that God knows the past and present in exhaustive detail but does not know the future in the same way. Sanders, *The God Who Risks,* 194. God's hesitancy about unsettled aspects of the future speaks to the issue of omniscience. Our definitions should flow from an integrated reading of the Bible and not be established on other grounds. Pinnock, *Most Moved Mover,* 64. God's knowledge of the world is also dynamic rather than static. Instead of perceiving the entire course of human existence in one timeless moment, God comes to know events as they take place. He learns something from what transpires. Rice, "Biblical Support for a New Perspective"; in Pinnock, *The Openness of God,* 16. Future-land is a region of fairytale. "The future" consists of certain actual trends and tendencies in the present that have not yet been fulfilled. . . . Ahead of where the Moving Finger has writ there is only blank paper; no X-ray vision can reveal what is going to stand there, any more than some scientific treatment of the paper on my desk can show what words I am going to inscribe on it. Geach, *Providence and Evil,* 52–53. The central idea concerning God's knowledge of the future . . . can be simply stated: God knows everything about the future which it is logically possible for him to know. Hasker, *God, Time, and Knowledge,* 187. [The open view] affirms that the future decisions of self-determining agents are only possibilities until agents freely actualize them. In this view, therefore, the future is partly comprised of possibilities. And since God knows all things perfectly—just as they are, and not otherwise—God knows the future as partly comprised of possibilities. Boyd, *Satan and the Problem of Evil,* 90–91.

Terms and Definitions

	Orthodoxy	Open Theism
Omnipresence	God may be said to be present with all things in three modes: (1) by power and operation; (2) by knowledge; (3) by essence. . . . He is said to be everywhere by his power because he produces and governs all things. . . . He is present with all by his knowledge because he sees and beholds all things. . . . He is everywhere by his essence because his essence penetrates all things and is wholly by itself intimately present with each and everything. Turretin, *Institutes of Elenctic Theology*, 1.3.9.4. The omnipresence of God . . . has been regarded as very difficult for speculative thought. . . . The doctrine of an infinite essence of being should be carefully guarded in both thought and expression. Otherwise it may become the foundation of pantheism. In all true theism the divine essence is pure, absolute spirit. All sense of magnitude or spatial extension is alien to such a nature, and should be excluded from our notion of the divine ubiquity. Miley, *Systematic Theology,* 1:217–18. . . . God can, while transcending space and time, enter spatial and temporal creatures without dislodging them, while still being omnipresent invisibly and spiritually in every place and time. Oden, *The Living God,* 60.	In speaking of creation, it must be clear that one is not saying that God and the world are distinct substances in the same sense, standing over against each other. . . . I can never be outside God; for he knows me directly and can cause me to cease to be at any moment; I exist only by his presence and power. God must be conceived as having direct knowledge of every created thing and the ability to act directly, in an unmediated way, on any created thing. This is the traditional doctrine of Divine omnipresence; and it can be pictorially expressed by saying that the world is the body of God. . . . Ward, *Rational Theology and the Creativity of God,* 83–84. Omnipresence describes God's involvement in the world spatially; it is the quality of being everywhere. . . . The characteristic of omnipresence raises the question of whether or not God has a body of some kind. . . . Those who believe that God has a body often appeal to the biblical statement that man was created "in the image of God" (Gen. 1:27), which seems to suggest a physical similarity between man and God. . . . In addition, many biblical passages attribute physical characteristics to God. . . . Those who affirm God's incorporeality usually interpret biblical passages which attribute physical characteristics to God as "anthropomorphisms." An anthropomorphism describes God as if he had human qualities. Rice, *The Reign of God,* 73–74. What is it for there to be an Omnipresent Spirit? . . . Clearly God is not supposed to be embodied. . . . There is no material object, in which disturbances cause God pains; nor any material object whose state affects the way in which God thinks about the world. . . . There is no one place from which God looks out on the world, yet he knows without inference about any state of the world. . . . Swinburne, *The Coherence of Theism,* 102–3. Presence has to do with relationship. The distance between those in the relationship decreases as they freely share themselves. Becoming close means being available and vulnerable. The relationship may backfire. One may be taken advantage of and hurt. In this regard it is not surprising that the divine presence is affected by human action. Sanders, *The God Who Risks,* 79.

Terms and Definitions

	Orthodoxy	Open Theism
Sovereignty	. . . God's moral government over mankind, his treating them as moral agents . . . is not inconsistent with a determining disposal of all events, of every kind, throughout the universe, in his providence; either by positive efficacy, or permission. Indeed such an *universal, determining providence,* infers some kind of necessity of all events; such a necessity as implies an infallible previous fixedness of the futurity of the event. . . . Edwards, *The Works of Jonathan Edwards: The Freedom of the Will,* 431. . . . God's foreknowledge is incompatible with human freedom . . . this does not involve a further consequence, logical fatalism. . . . The adverse consequences for human responsibility of denying indeterminism are considerably exaggerated. Helm, *Eternal God,* 127. . . . All [God's] wisdom is continually employed in managing all the affairs of his creation for the good of all his creatures. . . . To him all things are possible: He doeth whatsoever pleaseth him, in heaven and earth, and in the sea, and all deep places, and we cannot doubt of his exerting all his power, as in sustaining, so in governing, all that he has made. Wesley, *The Works of John Wesley,* VI.LXVII:317. The sovereignty of God may be defined as the exercise of His supremacy. . . . He is the Most High, Lord of heaven and earth. Subject to none, influenced by none, absolutely independent: God does as He pleases, only as He pleases, always as He pleases. None can thwart Him, none can hinder Him. . . . Divine sovereignty means that God is God in fact, as well as in name, that He is on the Throne of the universe, directing all things. . . . Pink, *The Attributes of God,* 32.	God cannot in [the Process] view meticulously control everything. There must be an element of unpredictability permeating all of reality. As I have noted in previous chapters, I agree with this perspective. Boyd, *Satan and the Problem of Evil,* 277. We cannot understand how [the disparity between God's will of decree and His wishes, or general intentions] could exist for the God who possesses exhaustive sovereignty. We conclude, then, that while it is hard (if not impossible) to imagine Calvinism without the distinction between God's sovereign will and his moral will, it is harder still to coherently conceive of a God in which this distinction really exists. Basinger, "Exhaustive Divine Sovereignty: A Practical Critique"; in Pinnock, *The Grace of God, The Will of Man,* 203. Though the Spirit may not get everything he desires, we have reason to hope because we have a God with a proven track record. . . . God has achieved some of what he wants, but much more remains to be accomplished. Sanders, *The God Who Risks,* 129. God is sovereign over his sovereignty and is thus free to choose what sorts of relations he desires to create. Sanders, *The God Who Risks,* 211. . . . God has sovereignly established a type of world in which God sets up general structures or an overall framework for meaning and allows the creatures significant input into exactly how things will turn out. . . . God macromanages the overall project (while remaining free to micromanage some things). . . . Sanders, *The God Who Risks,* 213. . . . General sovereignty denies that each and every event has a specific divine intention. God may intensify his ongoing activity to bring about some particular event, but God's normal way of operating is to allow the creatures significant freedom and, consequently, not to control everything. Sanders, *The God Who Risks,* 214. Within these general structures God permits things to happen, both good and bad, that he does not specifically intend. Yet God may act to bring about a specific event in order to bring the divine project to fruition. Sanders, *The God Who Risks,* 214.

Terms and Definitions

	Orthodoxy	Open Theism
Relationship to Creation	Creation did not produce a change in God, but in creatures. . . . When God became the Creator, he was not changed in himself (for nothing new happened to him, for from eternity he had the efficacious will of creating the world in time). . . . Turretin, *Institutes of Elenctic Theology*, 1.3.11.5. In his conception of creation Calvin definitely separated himself from all dualistic, and especially from all pantheistic elements of thought by sharply asserting that all substantial existence outside of God owes its being to God, that it was created by God out of nothing, and that it came from God's hand very good. Warfield, *Calvin and Calvinism,* 289. When God created the heavens and the earth, and all that is therein, at the conclusion of each day's work it is said, "And God saw that it was good." Whatever was created was good in its kind; suited to the end for which it was designed; adapted to promote the good of the whole, and the glory of the great Creator. Wesley, *The Works of John Wesley,* VI.LVI:206. . . . The church must draw a distinction between God's "ordinary [or "general"] providence" and his "special providence". . . . meaning by the former, for example, what the Psalmist extols God for in Psalm 145—that in love and tender compassion he sustains and cares for all his creatures (theologians speak of this as God's "common grace"), and by the latter those specific divine activities looking directly to the salvation of his elect (that is, his "special grace"). But one must be careful, when distinguishing between his ordinary ("common" or "general") and special providence, not to interpret these "kinds" of providence to mean that God is conducting *two* works alongside each other with no relationship between them. Scripturally, this simply is not so. . . . One must never sever any aspect of God's providence away from the . . . relationship that exists between God and his creation, since all of God's dealings with his creation are mediated through the Christ. To do so provides the natural theologian the ground he needs to conduct his theological enterprise with no thought, at least at first, of Christ the Creator and Sustainer of all things. The Scriptures will not permit such an enterprise, however, insisting that Christ is not only the Co-Creator with the Father and the Spirit of the universe, but its Sustainer as well. . . . Reymond, *A New Systematic Theology of the Christian Faith,* 399–400.	. . . If our understanding of nature is to be taken as a rediscovery of God's rational creating of nature . . . then we shall see nature to be more fully rational the less it is derivable deductively from first principles (as if God were simply a super-computer) and the more it is comprehensible as a product of creative insight and originality within a general structure of law. I propose that such a view gives more credit to God as a being of personal rationality, as a creator in the real sense, than the deterministic theories which can only view God as the sufficient cause of the world, determining all things as he must, with boring monotony. There is a place, then, for the indeterminate, the spontaneous, in an intelligible creation. Ward, *Rational Theology and the Creativity of God,* 155–56. It is evident that the view of God's governance of the world here proposed differs from others that are commonly held. . . . Does God make decisions that depend for their outcomes on the responses of free creatures in which the decisions themselves are not informed by knowledge of the outcomes? If he does, then creating and governing a world is for God a risky business. Hasker, *God, Time, and Knowledge,* 197. Condescension is involved in God's decision to make this kind of a world. By willing the existence of significant beings with independent status alongside of himself, God accepts limitations not imposed from without. Pinnock, *The Openness of God,* 113. . . . We cannot, in principle, fathom God apart from our relationship as creatures. We ought not speculate about what it means to be God. Instead, we must see what God actually decides to do in relation to the creation in order to know what it means to be God. Sanders, *The God Who Risks,* 41. . . . The creation is due to divine grace. God did not have to create. It is the divine wisdom in freedom that brings into existence something that is not God. Since the creation is contingent, not necessary, one cannot draw conclusions about the Creator from the nature of the creation without further ado. Sanders, *The God Who Risks,* 41. . . . God works within limits. For God to say yes to creating this particular world means that God had to say no (we think) to other possibilities. . . . God has sovereignly decided to create and work with this particular world rather than others. . . . God is the sovereign Creator, for there is no opposition to his act of creating. Sanders, *The God Who Risks,* 41.

PART TWO

Hermeneutics and Theological Language

Hermeneutics and Theological Language

	Orthodoxy	Open Theism
Concepts **Univocal** **Equivocal** **Analogical**	Only univocal assertions protect us from equivocacy; only univocal knowledge is, therefore, genuine and authentic knowledge. . . . Only a univocal element in analogical affirmation can save it from equivocation. Unless we have some literal truth about God, no similarity between man and God can in fact be predicated; the very possibility of analogy founders unless something is truly known about both analogates. The alternative to univocal knowledge of God is equivocation and skepticism. Henry, *God, Revelation and Authority,* 2:364 . . . We cannot know everything about God. There are undoubtedly mysteries about him which none of us understands. But we must recognize that this doesn't mean we know nothing about him whatsoever or that none of our claims, whether literal or figurative, are true. Feinberg, *No One Like Him,* 76. God's attributes differ from ours in that they are the source and standard of ours. . . . The fact that God's nature is the source and standard of ours does not prohibit, but rather makes possible, comparisons between God and ourselves. . . . The qualities of creatures resemble their divine standard in various degrees and ways, for the standard is a perfect person rather than an abstract concept. Frame, *The Doctrine of God,* 366. . . . There are two modes of this second perception from the works and the word of God. The First is that of Affirmation, (which is also styled by Thomas Aquinas, "the mode of Causality and by the habitude of the principle,") according to which the simple perfections which are in the creatures, as being the productions of God, are attributed analogically to God according to some similitude. Arminius, *Public Disputations,* IV.I God's way of loving is not wholly discontinuous with what we know of loving. . . . Although Jesus is realistic about the inadequacies of human love, he nonetheless invites us to think of God's care in comparison with good parental care. . . . [Wesley, *WJW* V, p. 333] Oden, *The Living God,* 120.	. . . [diverse] thinkers . . . all agree that there must be a "hard literal core" or "univocal core" to our talk about God. Sanders, *The God Who Risks,* 25. Our concepts of God are obviously inadequate; they will never do justice to the fullness of the divine reality. . . . But this doesn't mean that our concepts of God completely misrepresent him. Our ideas of God can, and should, be accurate as far as they go . . . even though we can't know everything about God, or even very much about him, we can know something. Rice, *The Reign of God,* 49. . . . A being who is not a subject or a member of a class or in any way complex cannot be described by language which refers to subjects by means of general class-descriptions, and which consists of many various and complex terms. The problem of analogy assumes the alarming proportions it does in Thomist theology because God is defined in such a way that no terms could possibly describe him. No simple, eternal being can be correctly described in complex nouns and tensed verbs. Ward, *Rational Theology and the Creativity of God,* 59. It is true that God lies forever beyond our powers of comprehension. His greatness surpasses all human descriptions. But to conclude that we should give up any attempt to understand him is a mistake. Rice, *The Reign of God,* 48. Some may find something odd about applying human concepts to God. Is this not making God in our image? But all the language we employ to speak of God is human language and thus is tinged with anthropomorphism. Those who have found this situation quite troubling have sought an escape. Sanders, *The God Who Risks,* 19–20. While no metaphor provides us with a literal account of the divine reality—a one-to-one correspondence to its object—this does not mean that all metaphors are equally distant from the object represented. Rice, "Biblical Support for a New Perspective"; in Pinnock, *The Openness of God,* 17.

Hermeneutics and Theological Language

	Orthodoxy	Open Theism
Predication **Univocal** **Equivocal** **Analogical**	The Bible . . . provides a basis for distinguishing between God's incommunicable attributes, that is, perfections that are predicable of God alone, and his communicable attributes, or divine perfections shared in some respects by his creatures. Henry, *God, Revelation and Authority,* V.1:99. . . . We make positive claims about God when we predicate moral attributes of him such as love and justice. . . . For metaphors about God to make sense, I must know some things about him that are both literal and true. Feinberg, *No One Like Him,* 76-77. If the difference between creator and creature means the same term cannot be predicated of both univocally, is it then used equivocally of them, i.e., in entirely different senses? Answering negatively, Aquinas explains that such language cannot be equivocal, "because if that were so, it follows that from creatures nothing at all could be known or demonstrated about God. . . ." Feinberg, *No One Like Him,* 78.	Anthropomorphic language does not preclude literal predication to God. Of course, the question must be asked, What is it to which the anthropomorphisms refer? If God shares the same context with us by entering into relation with us, as the biblical revelation presupposes, then we have a basis for our language about God. Sanders, *The God Who Risks,* 25. If human beings and God have nothing whatever in common, if we have utterly no mutual experience, then we have no way of talking and thinking about God and there is no possibility of a personal relationship with him. Rice, "Biblical Support for a New Perspective"; in Pinnock, *The Openness of God,* 35. There is not always a one-for-one correspondence in texts that tell us important things. In any analogy there is something literal about reality that we don't want to miss and, at the same time, something different. Pinnock, *Most Moved Mover,* 62.
Predication **Univocal**	. . . It makes sense to speak of a timeless knower's foreknowledge of events where the notion of foreknowledge expresses a temporal knower's belief or recognition that certain events were known timelessly before this time. But to say this is not to claim that the timeless knower's knowledge is analogical or anthropomorphic. It is literally knowledge, and it is literally foreknowledge, but it is not foreknowledge for the timeless knower. Helm, *Eternal God,* 101. We need not be afraid of saying that some of our language about God is univocal or literal. God has given us language that literally applies to him. When one says negatively that "God is not a liar," no word in that sentence is analogous or figurative. The sentence distinguishes God from literal liars, not analogous ones. Similarly, the statement that "God is good" uses the term *good* univocally. God's goodness is, of course, different from ours in important ways. But goodness on either the divine or the human level can be defined by such concepts as justice, mercy, and kindness. The differences between God's nature and ours do not require that we use the term *good* in different senses. Frame, *The Doctrine of God,* 209. . . . For metaphors about God to make sense, I must know some things about him that are both literal and true. Feinberg, *No One Like Him,* 77.	It's difficult to conceive of how God could be more explicit. The fact that verses as explicit as these aren't allowed to communicate that God really changes his mind or experiences regret or unexpected disappointment testifies to the truth that the classical exegesis of these passages is driven by philosophy rather than by the texts. Boyd, *God of the Possible,* 86. . . . It seems much better to take the Bible at its word and to understand God as a temporal being. Hasker, "A Philosophical Perspective"; in Pinnock, *The Openness of God,* 128. There must be some properties that are used of God in the same sense that they are used of things in the created order. . . . Anthropomorphic language does not preclude literal predication to God. Sanders, *The God Who Risks,* 25. We can accept at face value the biblical statements that attribute powerful emotions to God. We do not have to dismiss them as "anthropomorphisms" or "anthropopathisms," which have no application to his real life. The open view of God does justice to a broad spectrum of biblical evidence and allows for a natural reading of the Bible. Rice, "Biblical Support for a New Perspective"; in Pinnock, *The Openness of God,* 49.

Hermeneutics and Theological Language

	Orthodoxy	Open Theism
Predication Equivocal	. . . For example, the property of being omniscient is usually regarded as being essential to God and as not being possessed or possessable by anything distinct from God. It is a property unique to God and essential to him. Helm, *Eternal God,* 208. How does the distinction between essential and accidental attributes relate to God? Theologians and philosophers within the Judaeo-Christian tradition have maintained that all of God's attributes are essential attributes. Unlike his creatures, God has no accidental predicates. Remove or change any of God's attributes and there would be no God. Feinberg, *No One Like Him,* 234. Whatsoever things are predicated absolutely concerning God, they belong to Him from all eternity and all together. It is certain that those things which do not from all eternity belong to Him, are predicated about Him not absolutely, but in reference to the creatures, such as, "He is the Creator, the Lord, the Judge of all men." Arminius, *Public Disputations,* IV.XIV	It is one thing to assert that God does not share all properties with anything else, but it is quite another matter to say that God does not share any properties with anything else. . . . If "infinite" means without any predicates from within the confines of the conditions of our existence (all human language and conceptualizing), then we are committed to agnosticism about *anything transcendent*—not just God! . . . If the qualitative difference between God and humanity is absolutely *infinite*, then there is no correspondence between God and the creation. . . . Thus it would seem that those who affirm that God shares no properties with anything in the created order are committed to silence concerning anything transcendental. . . . Sanders, *The God Who Risks,* 29.
Predication Analogical	. . . What I am suggesting is that "God" may be thought to express the individual essence of God and this consists in a set of properties some of which are shareable (other individuals than God may have them) but the set of which is unique to him. Helm, *Eternal God,* 208. Is biblical revelation about God univocal or analogical? Can we know God as he is in himself, or is an analogical comprehension the most we can hope for? The difference is this: A given predicate applied to different subjects *univocally* would intend that the subjects possess the predicate in a precisely identical sense. The opposite of univocality is equivocality, which attaches a given predicate to separate subjects in a completely different or unrelated sense. Now lying between univocality and equivocality is analogy. A predicate employed *analogically* intends a relationship between separate subjects based upon comparison or proportion. Reymond, *A New Systematic Theology of the Christian Faith,* 96.	The alternative to supposing that theology uses familiar words in their normal senses is to suppose that it gives to old words a new sense; that "wise", "powerful", "person", etc. are given new senses in their introduction into theology. Now quite obviously such words are not given entirely new senses in such a case. . . . That being so, the process of giving a new sense to old words must take the form of amending the meaning of old words. Swinburne, *The Coherence of Theism,* 54–55. . . . God repents, but not as humans do; God suffers, but not exactly as we do; God works out his purposes in time, but not subject to the ravages of time as we are. I do not take every biblical metaphor literally but I do try to take them all seriously. I especially do not want to diminish the reality of God's involvement in time and space and the intimacy of his relationship with us. Pinnock, *Most Moved Mover,* 62.

Hermeneutics and Theological Language

	Orthodoxy	Open Theism
Anthropomorphic Language **Anthropo-morphism** **Anthropopoiesis** **Anthropopathism**	A more theocentric point of view than most of us habitually adopt in thinking about God would allow us to think of God accommodating himself to human time-bound and space-bound modes of thought, as he must be thought by all theists (or at least all theists who recognize a divine revelation) to accommodate himself to human powers of visual or other imagery in the use of what are traditionally called anthropomorphisms. Helm, *Eternal God,* 108. Emotions in human beings often have physical accompaniments and symptoms. . . . Since God is incorporeal . . . his emotions are not like ours in that respect. . . . But God's incorporeality gives us no reason to deny in some general way that God has emotions. Frame, *The Doctrine of God,* 610. What then is meant by the term repentance? The very same that is meant by the other forms of expression, by which God is described to us humanly. Because our weakness cannot reach his height, any description which we receive of him must be lowered to our capacity in order to be intelligible. And the mode of lowering is to represent him not as he really is, but as we conceive of him. Calvin, *Institutes,* 1.17.13. But may not such representations of God be anthropomorphic (or anthropochronic) in order to render his relations to his creation more intelligible to us? For it is agreed that there are anthropomorphisms in the Bible. God does not have ears, or a mouth; indeed he does not have a face, or feet, or a body of any kind. But anthropomorphism must stop somewhere, and while it is patent that God cannot have an ear . . . it is not so obvious that he cannot be a spirit in time who represents himself, for vividness and convenience, as having a body. References to God being in space are anthropomorphic while references to him being in time are, apparently, not anthropomorphic. Helm, *Eternal God,* 2–3. To call God a rock, a shepherd, or a consuming fire, or to say that Jesus is the door, is using language not literally but metaphorically. Moreover, if we grant that God is pure spirit, when writers speak of the "hand of God," "the eyes of God," "the face of the Lord," their claims are anthropomorphic. . . . Feinberg, *No One Like Him,* 77.	The classical-philosophical theistic tradition has judged all of this scriptural talk to be anthropomorphic. It has had to, not because anything in Scripture suggests this but because of a nonbiblical philosophical presupposition. . . . This hermeneutic amounts to an illegitimate exaltation of what is taken to be general revelation over special revelation. In essence it says: since we know (from Hellenistic philosophy!) that God is immutable, timeless, impassible, purely actual, devoid of contingency and so on, these passages cannot mean what they seem to mean. Boyd, *God at War,* 130. If physical descriptions of the divine reality are not to be taken literally, is the same true of descriptions of God as deliberating, deciding, acting and feeling? To avoid turning God into an enlarged human being, must we deny not only that God shares our physical properties but our intellectual, volitional and emotional properties too? Rice, "Biblical Support for a New Perspective"; in Pinnock, *The Openness of God,* 34–35. The other irony surfaces when Christians disparage anthropomorphism, since Jesus is the consummate anthropomorphism. If Jesus is God incarnate, then it does not seem that God is especially concerned about having human characteristics predicated of him. Sanders, *The God Who Risks,* 21. . . . The term *anthropomorphism* may have a narrow or broad meaning. The narrow, and customary, sense refers to speaking of God as having human characteristics such as emotions or eyes. Anthropomorphism, however, is sometimes used more broadly in the sense that all our language about God is *human language.* When speaking of God, whether we use abstract terms such as *necessity* and *aseity* or concrete terms such as *lover* and *rock,* we are inevitably predicating properties of God that are derived from human categories. When humans use language, it is *human* language that we use to speak about anything—from God to black holes. Sanders, *The God Who Risks,* 22. The Fathers . . . viewed any biblical references to God's emotions, repentance, etc. as "mere" anthropomorphisms. They were for the benefit of . . . those who could not comprehend the true nature of God. Sanders, "God as Personal", in Pinnock, *The Grace of God, The Will of Man,* 167.

PART THREE

The Doctrine of Scripture in Open Theism

The Doctrine of Scripture in Open Theism

	Orthodoxy	Open Theism
Inerrancy	The question is not whether the sacred writers . . . could err. . . . Rather the question is whether in writing they were so acted upon and inspired by the Holy Spirit . . . as to be kept free from all error. . . . Our adversaries deny this; we affirm it. Turretin, *Institutes of Elenctic Theology*, 1.2.4.5. It seems at least to be made tolerably clear by such instances, that if we embark on the attempt to determine how much credit we ought to give the Bible by first attempting to settle in detail how much credit it is easy to give it, we may arrive at a harbor very different from that towards which we fancied we were bound. . . . [The Old Testament critics'] starting point is the assertion of errors in the text of Scripture; errors as determined by them in the use of an exegesis which scorns all "harmonizing expedients"—that is, which refuses to allow to Scripture what every historian feels necessary to allow to his sources. Warfield, *Limited Inspiration,* 46. The Holy Scriptures are one source, and by all pre-eminence the source, of theology. . . . That they are a direct revelation from God, with the seal of a divine original clearly set upon them, gives to their theology a certainty and sufficiency . . . specially divine. Miley, *Systematic Theology*, 1:12.	The notion that God could be dismayed or wrong about anything may not sit well with some people, so perhaps some qualifications may be helpful. First, what is meant by the word mistake? . . . Even if we affirm that God is sometimes "mistaken" in the sense that God believed something would happen when, in fact, it does not come about, there is a question as to how often this happens. The biblical record gives a few occasions, but we are in no position to judge just how many times this occurs with God. Even if it happens regularly, this does not imply that God is helpless in the face of the future. . . . Sanders, *The God Who Risks*, 132–33. There are many other ways in which the Bible portrays God as facing a partly open future. Hear the frustration of the Lord, for example, as he expresses his amazement at Israel's stubbornness. . . . How could the Lord *genuinely think* that Israel would do one thing if in fact he eternally foreknew that Israel would not do this? The Lord's expression of disappointment can be authentic only if the future partly consists of possibilities and probabilities, not exclusively settled certainties. Boyd, *Satan and the Problem of Evil,* 100–101. Passages such as these need not imply that God was caught off guard, as though he didn't anticipate the *possibility* of the improbable. Nor do they imply that God was mistaken in thinking people would do one thing when it turns out they did another. . . . The omniscient Lord, having a perfectly accurate assessment of all probabilities, *thought* his people would do [one thing]. . . . But many of his people, being self-determining free creatures, opted for the more improbable course of action. Boyd, *Satan and the Problem of Evil,* 101. . . . The concept of inerrancy is itself unbiblical. Nowhere do the writers of the Bible assert that all their statements are inerrant. Those who adhere to this idea have deduced it from their concept of divine inspiration and imposed it on the Bible. Rice, *The Reign of God,* 33.

The Doctrine of Scripture in Open Theism

	Orthodoxy	Open Theism
Predictive Prophecy	The prophets did not fall into mistakes in those things which they wrote as inspired men . . . not even in the smallest particulars. . . . Turretin, *Institutes of Elenctic Theology,* 1.2.4.23. Barr's reticence concerning predictive prophecy seems to rise especially from two considerations. First of all, he contends, "prediction and fulfillment" carry "serious philosophical consequences"—as indeed they do. Barr declares specifically that "exact knowledge of distant future events" implies divine "determinism" and would involve "a mechanical or dictation view of inspiration. . . ." Yet evangelical theology has long and repeatedly emphasized that the inspired prophets do not need to be mechanically computerized in order to relay truly what God was saying through them. And if, to avoid an objectionable determinism, we must insist that God is either ignorant, confused or silent about the future, we are postulating a god very different from the God of the Bible. Henry, *God, Revelation and Authority,* IV.3:347–48. When [a true prophet's] prophecies predict future events, God's word gives him supernatural knowledge. If the event does not happen, the prophet is proved false. Deuteronomy 18 does not consider the possibility that God himself may have been in error. . . . Moses presupposes that God himself is omniscient and cannot err in foretelling the future. The text banishes from the outset any consideration that God might be wrong. Frame, *The Doctrine of God,* 487. Prediction of future events is not the only aspect of prophecy. . . . Nevertheless, amid the diverse elements of prophecy, one crucial element is prediction of the future. Knowledge of the future is a defining mark of the true God and of his true prophets. Frame, *The Doctrine of God,* 487–88.	God is yet working to fulfill his promises and bring his project to fruition. The eschaton will surprise us because it is not set in concrete; it is not unfolding according to a prescribed script. Sanders, *The God Who Risks,* 125. Predictions are very specific forecasts of what is to occur, whereas prophecies allow room for God to fulfill them in a variety of ways—ways that we cannot anticipate. . . . Despite the messianic prophecies, no one anticipated the sort of messiahship that Jesus exhibited. Sanders, *The God Who Risks,* 126. The promises of God should be understood as part of the divine *project* rather than as some eternal blueprint, a project in which God has not scripted the way everything in human history will go. God has a goal, but the routes remain open. Sanders, *The God Who Risks,* 127. Can God be mistaken about anything? If God can be mistaken about what will happen in the future, then divine predictions may be in doubt. . . . Is it possible for God to have mistaken beliefs about the future? The traditional theological answer is that God cannot, but there are several biblical texts that seem to affirm that what God thought would happen did not come about. . . . Sanders, *The God Who Risks,* 205. Some claim that certain predictions entail exhaustive divine foreknowledge and prevent us from appealing to the evidence that suggests limited prescience. Biblical prophecy is a complex phenomenon, but does not entail any such thing. . . . Some prophecies are conditional, leaving the future open, and, presumably, God's knowledge of it. Pinnock, *Most Moved Mover,* 50. It is very meaningful to think of the future as partly settled and partly unsettled because it tells us that not everything has been decided at this point in time. It means that the future is a realm of possibilities not just of actualities. This is true even for God. . . . Pinnock, *Most Moved Mover,* 51.

The Doctrine of Scripture in Open Theism

	Orthodoxy	Open Theism
Inspiration	Defining inspiration positively, it may be described as the influence of the Holy Spirit upon a human person, whereby he is infallibly moved and guided in all his statements while under this influence. Shedd, *Dogmatic Theology*, 1:88. . . . In the only passage where the word Inspiration is used in Scripture, it is ascribed not to the prophet but to Scripture itself: "Every Scripture is inspired of God" (2 Tim. iii. 16). . . . It is a common locution in the New Testament by which Scripture is assigned to the Holy Spirit as its responsible author. Warfield, *Limited Inspiration,* 11. Inspiration is a supernatural influence. It is thus distinguished, on the one hand, from the providential agency of God, which is everywhere and always in operation; and on the other hand, from the gracious operations of the Spirit on the hearts of his people. . . . Inspiration belongs to the . . . class [of those effects produced by God's immediate efficiency without the intervention of secondary causes]. . . . Inspiration, therefore, is not to be confused with spiritual illumination. Hodge, *Systematic Theology,* 1.6.2. The Church has never held what has been stigmatized as the mechanical theory of inspiration. The sacred writers were not machines. Their self-consciousness was not suspended; nor were their intellectual powers superceded. Holy men spake as they were moved by the Holy Ghost. . . . God uses his instruments according to their nature. The sacred writers impressed their peculiarities on their several productions as plainly as though they were the subjects of no extraordinary influence. . . . Nevertheless, and none the less, they spoke as they were moved by the Holy Ghost, and their words were his words. Hodge, *Systematic Theology*, 1.6.2. In Scripture we are dealing with what the Holy Spirit tells and foretells, with divinely inspired data, with what is known by special revelation, with what the Spirit communicates in a definitive way. God is the authority who renders Scripture authoritative; inspiration is the special phenomenon that imparts this character of divine authority to the writings and logically necessitates fulfillment of written prophecies. Henry, *God, Revelation and Authority*, IV.3:75.	My basic position is that we have it on Christ's authority, which itself can be established on solid historical grounds, *that* Scripture is divinely inspired, but next to nothing as to *how* Scripture is divinely inspired. Hence, though I defend the inspiration and infallibility of Scripture, I am in principle completely open to the historical-critical investigation of the particular historical processes by which various segments of Scripture came about. In my view, an unequivocal affirmation of scriptural inspiration does not entail anything in the direction of the "divine dictation theory" espoused by some American fundamentalists. Boyd, *God at War,* 300 n.37. . . . The biblical doctrine of "inspiration" contains two important ideas. One is the divine authority of Scripture. The prophets, the writers of the Bible, did not speak or write on their own initiative; their messages originated with God. Moreover, God guides in the transmission of these messages to ensure that what is heard and read is the reliable expression of his will. A second implication of inspiration is the divine-human character of Scripture. The message comes from God, but it is expressed in human terms and concepts, and the different writings clearly reflect the personalities of the authors. Rice, *The Reign of God,* 25–26. Although the new theology of inspiration may only be a cloud the size of a human hand, there are forces at work which favor it over the stricter view. One is the simple practical bent of the evangelical style of faith, which believes strongly in the values of faith at work in mission and action, and shies away from intellectualism and abstraction. After all, the new evangelical view which dispenses with inerrancy is less a retreat from a high position on the authority of the Bible, than a move toward greater doctrinal *simplicity.* What most evangelicals want to know is how they can trust and use the Scriptures available to them, despite difficulties that crop up through transmission, translation, or inherently. How can Scripture be a lamp to their feet and a light to their path? Such a question has little to do with the perfect errorlessness of non-existent autographs and a great deal to do with the continuing authority of a (slightly) imperfect document. Pinnock, "Evangelicals and Inerrancy: The Current Debate," *Theology Today* 35.1 (1978).

PART FOUR

Historical Understandings of Ultimate Reality and God

Historical Understandings of Ultimate Reality and God

	Greek Philosophers	
	Quotes from Orthodox Theologians	**Quotes from Openness Theologians**
Parmenides	The Eleatic philosopher Parmenides (c. 475 B.C.) totally denied the reality of becoming. . . . and declared that immutable being is the first principle and, indeed, all there is. Henry, *God, Revelation and Authority,* V.1:44. . . . the very idea of change bewildered Parmenides. For him, change always implies something appearing out of what is not. But something cannot come from nothing. So Parmenides taught that there is no change. Change is an illusion; the world is really unchanging. Frame, *The Doctrine of God,* 559. How did the idea of atemporal duration become part of Christian theology? . . . As to the origin of the idea of atemporal eternity . . . Kneale traces [it] to Parmenides. . . . Feinberg, *No One Like Him,* 379–80.	. . . Parmenides held that "being," the One, is eternally full and complete and so is unchangeable. He also introduced the definition of eternity as timelessness. The One is "uncreated and imperishable, for it is entire, immovable and without end. It was not in the past, nor shall it be, since it is now, all at once." [G. S. Kirk and J. E. Raven, *The Presocratic Philosophers* (New York: Cambridge University Press, 1962), p. 273.] Sanders, "Historical Considerations"; in Pinnock, *The Openness of God,* 62. Parmenides argued that there is only what is; so it must be mere words to speak of past and future. . . . Geach, *Providence and Evil,* 53–54.
Heraclitus	Instead of acknowledging God as living and transcendent, Greek philosophers—notably Heraclitus and the Stoics—tended to equate God simply with the living essence of the world. Henry, *God, Revelation and Authority,* V.1:68 Heraclitus began with the proposition that everything changes. But if everything changes, how can we identify something long enough to talk about it? . . . Heraclitus answered that although everything changes, it does so according to a rational pattern, which he called the *logos*. . . . Frame, *The Doctrine of God,* 559–60. As to the philosophical background of the classical model [of God], ancient Greek philosophers were concerned to find some element of stability in a world where everything seemed to be changing and in the process of becoming. Heraclitus argued that all of reality is in a state of flux, but that thought was unsettling to the Greek mind. Feinberg, *No One Like Him,* 63.	We have been shifting from a static to a thoroughly dynamic understanding of reality. For example, the Platonic notion that time and change were less real than timeless stability is being abandoned in light of the discovery that many of the world's fundamental processes are unidirectional and irreversible. Increasingly, physicists and others are working on the assumption that time is real. [See P. Coveney and R. Highfield, *The Arrow of Time* (New York: Fawcett Columbine, 1990).] Boyd, *God of the Possible,* 107. In short, the old assumption that the world is a stable, solid, deterministic, thoroughly rational, and utterly predictable system has been replaced by a view of the world as a dynamic process that is to some extent indeterministic and unpredictable. Boyd, *God of the Possible,* 108.

Historical Understandings of Ultimate Reality and God

	Greek Philosophers	
	Quotes from Orthodox Theologians	**Quotes from Openness Theologians**
Pythagoras	RELIGIOUS PHILOSOPHY has often considered infinity an attribute essential to any ideal conception of deity. . . . The first Greek philosopher to speculate on the concept of infinity, Anaximander, meant by the infinite (*to apeiron*) a limitless or inexhaustible substance that fuses nature's basic elements, a substance eternal, internally undivided, but having no definite quality. . . . The Pythagoreans somewhat modified this conception by postulating a limit *(peras)* that gives structure to the infinite. . . . Henry, *God, Revelation and Authority,* V.1:219.	
Plato	Carrying forward Philo's understanding of the Hebrew-Christian scriptures, some neo-Platonists tried to find fuller points of contact between the Christian revelation and philosophical theology. Philo . . . identified the biblical Logos with the Ideas that Plato had considered the formative principles of all existence. Henry, *God, Revelation and Authority,* V.1:199. It is true that medieval theologians were aware of the teaching of certain Greek philosophers in discussing God's immutability. . . . They noted Plato's argument that change in a supremely perfect being constitutes corruption, deterioration and loss of perfection. . . . The fact is, however, that the Hebrew-Christian belief in God's immutability arose independently of Greek philosophy; it stemmed from revelational sources rather than from speculative conjecture. Henry, *God, Revelation and Authority,* V.1:286. . . . Plato, the philosopher who first drew attention to eternal objects, did not give a definitive answer as to how they are related to God. In some writings, he seemed to teach that God is subordinate to the forms *[Timaeus]*. But in other places, he hinted that the forms depend in some way on God [*Republic*, bks 6 & 7]. During the first century A.D., the Jewish Platonist, Philo, somewhat ambiguously suggested that the eternal objects were thoughts of God. Nash, *The Concept of God,* 96.	Now the "God" Plato speaks of in his writings is different in several respects from the Christian God; nevertheless, [Plato's] argument could easily be used by a Christian to argue that the God of Christianity is immutable. Davis, *Logic and the Nature of God,* 41. In Plato's Timaeus . . . God fashions existing matter like a potter fashions clay. In contrast, "The Mosaic view implies that the world was created out of what did not already exist. . . . [It] implies that matter came into existence only at the time of creation and did not exist prior to creation." [Citing Robert L. Wilken, *The Christians as the Romans Saw Them* (New Haven: Yale University Press, 1984), p. 89.] This is the idea that *creatio ex nihilo* came to express. It means that the world's existence is due entirely to God's decision. God creates because God chooses to create. God's relations to the world are based on freedom, not on necessity. Pinnock, *Searching for an Adequate God,* 90. . . . I knew we had to clarify what we meant by the divine immutability. I saw that we have been far too influenced by Plato's idea that a perfect being would not change because, being perfect, it would not need to change—any change would be for the worse. The effect of this piece of Greek natural theology on Christian thinking had been to picture God as virtually incapable of responsiveness. Pinnock, "From Augustine to Arminius: A Pilgrimage in Theology"; in *The Grace of God, the Will of Man,* 24.

Historical Understandings of Ultimate Reality and God

	Greek Philosophers	
	Quotes from Orthodox Theologians	**Quotes from Openness Theologians**
Plato	Now there has been a long debate as to the definition of eternity as a divine attribute. The Greek philosophers Parmenides, Plato, and Plotinus understood "eternal" reality to be timeless—beyond or outside time. For Parmenides' Being, Plato's Forms, and Plotinus's One, there is no change, no before or after. Frame, *The Doctrine of God,* 545. After Heraclitus, philosophers generally tried to identify something constant, something unchanging in the world of change. For Plato, it was the world of Forms. For Aristotle, it was . . . his god, the great Unmoved Mover. For Plotinus, it was the One. Frame, *The Doctrine of God,* 560. As for the traditional Christian conception of God, process theists don't like the amount of power and control over our world that classical theism gives God. . . . In addition, traditional theism is said to rely on the metaphysics of ancient Greek philosophers, especially Plato and Aristotle. According to these Greeks, there are two types of reality. On the one hand, there is the present world of becoming, time, change, and real relations. On the other, there is another "world of timeless, changeless, and unrelated being, which is alone 'real' in the full sense of the word and so alone worthy of the epithet 'divine.' " [Quoting Shubert Ogden, "Toward a New Theism," p. 179.] Feinberg, *No One Like Him*, 153. . . . Plato and those of his school acknowledge indeed that God is uncreated and the Father and Maker of all things, but then they maintain that matter as well as God is uncreated, and aver that it is *coeval with God.* But if God is uncreated and matter uncreated, God is no longer, according to the Platonists, the Creator of all things, nor so far as their opinions hold, is the monarchy of God established. [Citing Theophilus, *To Autolycus* II.4, *ANF* II, p. 95, italics added.] Oden, *The Living God*, 250.	The idea of God's impassibility arises more from Plato than from the Bible. Pinnock, *The Openness of God,* 118. Philo defined the divine essence as "that which is." This is a non-revelational term that displaces the personal God of the biblical revelation and causes God's attributes to acquire meanings they would not otherwise have had. Pinnock, *Most Moved Mover,* 69. The influence of Philo, the Alexandrian Jewish philosopher, on the early patristic tradition was immense. He showed them how to interpret the Bible in the manner of middle Platonism. Pinnock, *Most Moved Mover,* 71 n. 20. Plato's "argument from perfection" (any change for a perfect being is always a change for the worse) is the standard means of arriving at divine immutability. This is true even of evangelicals who pride themselves on doing "biblical" rather than "natural" theology. Sanders, *The God Who Risks,* 186. [Plato's] notion of perfection carries with it several related ideas. First, Plato says that incarnations of the gods are impossible, as that would imply change. Hence, we must reject the writings of the poets about visitations of the gods. Second, God is a most blessed and happy being experiencing no "joy or sorrow or pleasure." [*Philebus* 33.] God is beyond such emotions, as they would disturb the perfection of his soul. Moreover, God does not love *(eros),* for one loves only what one lacks, and God lacks nothing. [*Symposium* 200–203.] A self-sufficient being has no need of love. Sanders, "Historical Considerations"; in Pinnock, *The Openness of God,* 63. . . . from Plato, Aristotle and the subsequent Hellenistic tradition, the church arrived at the notion that God was altogether unmoved, impassible, immutable, nontemporal and purely actual. Boyd, *God at War,* 67.

Historical Understandings of Ultimate Reality and God

	Greek Philosophers	
	Quotes from Orthodox Theologians	**Quotes from Openness Theologians**
Aristotle	The Prime Mover and formal cause of all change in the world, [Aristotle] said, is itself unmoved (*The Works of Aristotle: Metaphysics*, Book 4, 256a). Aristotle's philosophy, in which the Unmoved Mover coexists with a world of change in passage from potentiality to actuality, is sometimes said to anticipate the "open future" affirmed by contemporary process theology. Yet Aristotle's determinism in no way regards the world, as a whole, to be evolutionary; Aristotle considers the same species to have always existed. . . . [Aristotle also] resisted any view of dynamic process in which change is the very essence of reality and constantly transforms itself into what is qualitatively different. Henry, *God, Revelation and Authority,* V.1:45. The view of a timeless God is routinely disparaged by its critics as an unfortunate legacy of Greek philosophy, one that they consider incompatible with the biblical view of God; the Greeks, it is often said, were disinterested in time, whereas the God of the Bible is vitally concerned with both time and history. But Aristotle's extended discussion (*Physics,* Book IV, 218a–224a) shows that he was, indeed, interested in time. What the Greeks lacked was a metaphysical interest in the course of time. . . . Henry, *God, Revelation and Authority,* V.1:240. Some of the implications that follow from Aristotle's doctrine of pure form are obviously difficult to reconcile with the Christian doctrine of God. For one thing, Aristotle taught that God cannot think about anything in the changing and imperfect world. The only perfect thing worthy of God's attention is God Himself. For Aristotle's God to think about anything else would detract from His perfection. Aristotle's Unmoved Mover whose only activity is contemplation of his own nature is a far cry from the loving God described in the Bible. Nash, *The Concept of God,* 20–21.	[Aristotle's] unmoved mover is an immaterial substance whose being is pure actuality and possesses no potentiality. Since matter is corruptible and changeable God is immaterial, and since to have potential is to be susceptible to change God must have only actuality. This God is absolutely immutable. It also follows that this God cannot be affected by any other being (impassible) since he has no room for change. . . . This self-thinking thought is so radically independent (aseity) and is such pure actuality that it cannot *receive* the knowledge of other beings. To receive anything would imply dependency and deficiency. Sanders, "Historical Considerations"; in Pinnock, *The Openness of God,* 65–66. Aristotle's supreme God is unaware of the existence of the world and certainly has no need of entering into relations with others. [To know anything external entails a need for the object, which means that the knower is less than perfectly self-sufficient. See his *Eudemian Ethics* 7. Yet in criticizing Empedocles he implies that divine perfection includes knowledge of all that exists (*Metaphysics* 1000b)!] "Since he is in need of nothing God cannot have need of friends, nor will he have any." [*Eudemian Ethics* 1244b; *Nicomachean Ethics* 1159a.] God is literally apathetic toward the world as he has no concern or feelings toward it. God does not interact with the world nor enter into covenantal relations with humans—God only "contemplates." [*Nicomachean Ethics* 1178b.] God is neither providential nor righteous in regard to the world: "God is not an imperative ruler." [*Eudemian Ethics* 1249b.] Sanders, "Historical Considerations"; in Pinnock, *The Openness of God,* 66. Aristotle had maintained that anything that enters into relation with another being enters a reciprocal relationship and becomes dependent on that being. But Philo claims that though God's self-sufficiency cannot allow reciprocal relations, God's activities produce effects on the world that are not true relations but "quasi relations." Sanders, "Historical Considerations"; in Pinnock, *The Openness of God,* 70.

Historical Understandings of Ultimate Reality and God

	Greek Philosophers	
	Quotes from Orthodox Theologians	**Quotes from Openness Theologians**
Aristotle	First, we will consider the concept of creation *ex nihilo,* "out of nothing." But what does it mean that God created the universe out of nothing? . . . We must oppose both the Aristotelian notion of an eternal "matter" and the Platonic notion of an eternal "receptacle." Plato and Aristotle themselves understood to some extent the problems of accounting for the world by positing preexistent realities. . . . Both Plato's "receptacle" and Aristotle's "matter" are receivers of form, and so are essentially unformed, and therefore in one sense nonbeing. Frame, *The Doctrine of God,* 298–99. Aristotle argued that [God] must be fully in being (perfect) without any potentiality unrealized. If there were potency in the unmoved mover, he would not necessarily be self-sufficient. . . . For Aristotle . . . every existing thing except God is a combination of actuality and potentiality. Hence, they can and do grow and change. However, Aristotle reasoned that potentiality is an imperfection, for whatever has potentiality is not fully the being it might be. Aristotle . . . concluded that since God is a perfect being, he must be totally actual with no potentiality to become anything more than he is. Feinberg, *No One Like Him,* 63–64. The history of theism is plagued by errors caused by overemphasizing a single one or set of attributes while neglecting others. Aristotle stressed God's absolute essence, aseity (underived existence), self-contemplation, transcendence, and immutability, yet failed to grasp God's relationality, closeness, and covenant love toward humanity. [Aristotle, *Metaphysics,* BWA, pp. 689ff.] Oden, *The Living God,* 38.	Another concept often incorporated into the images of [God as] King and Author is omnipotence. Since God has literally all the power in the universe, God will get whatever he wants. This unlimited power effectually brings about whatever God knows. Plato and Aristotle were among the first to develop these notions of God. Using the method of natural theology, they began with the human concept of perfection and simply deduced the implications. Sanders, "God as Personal"; in Pinnock, *The Grace of God, the Will of Man,* 170. [With respect to God's experience of the world] the Christian view of God differs sharply from other ideas. For example, many Greek philosophers, such as Aristotle, believed that God is totally indifferent to the world. In their view the creaturely world is unworthy of God's attention, so he exists in the splendid isolation of eternity, where he thinks of nothing but himself. [Aristotle, *Metaphysics,* Book XII, chapters 6–9.] Rice, *The Reign of God,* 83. It was Aristotle, however, who was to be the philosophical mentor of later Christian theology. . . . [Aristotle] does propound a doctrine of God as . . . so self-sufficient that he depends on nothing other than himself in any respect. So, whatever it knows, it must know by inspection of itself alone. Ward, *Rational Theology and the Creativity of God,* 212–13. . . . Aristotle thought that the world always had existed and always would exist. Christian revelation had shown that the world had a beginning and would have an end in time. But even if . . . Aristotle had been right, that would not mean that the world was eternal in the sense in which God is eternal. Swinburne, *The Coherence of Theism,* 216. In Scripture, therefore, as opposed to the dominant Hellenistic philosophical tradition that so influenced the apologists and especially Augustine, there was nothing "heavenly" about being timeless, immutable, purely actual and devoid of contingency. Boyd, *God at War,* 141.

Historical Understandings of Ultimate Reality and God

	Greek Philosophers	
	Quotes from Orthodox Theologians	**Quotes from Openness Theologians**
Plotinus	Outside the Bible God's reality was frequently exposited in terms of abstract "Being." Certain ancient Greek philosophers, particularly Plotinus, characterized the Ultimate as beyond all limitation and predication, hence without identifiable attributes. Henry, *God, Revelation and Authority,* V.1:28. In the bible there are no definitions of time. In contrast to, say, Philo . . . or Plotinus no biblical writer says what time is not. . . . So it is impossible, Barr avers, to contrast Hebrew thought with Greek. . . . Helm, *Eternal God,* 6. . . . The [notion that we can't make any positive predications of God, only negative ones] has a long tradition in philosophy going back at least to the ancient Greek philosopher Plotinus. Feinberg, *No One Like Him,* 76. In reality, God is a being without any multiplicity at all, a simple being for whom any language suggesting complexity, distinctions, or multiplicity, is entirely unsuited. That is essentially the Neoplatonic view of Plotinus, in which the best name of God is One. Even that name is inadequate, however, since God is utterly beyond the descriptive power of human language. Frame, *The Doctrine of God,* 227. That God is willing to experience concretely our human alienations, sorrows, suffering, and death is quite different from philosophical concepts of transcendence and immanence. Hence philosophical idealisms from Plotinus to Hegel have stood somewhat aghast or dumbstruck by the triune mystery . . . at times attempting to include it within their "systems." Oden, *The Living God,* 221–22.	[For Philo] The true God is anonymous while the biblical God is named, and so the biblical God must refer only to God's activities and not to the essence of God. [This is the "God beyond God" so popular in writers from Plotinus to Tillich.] Hence, the God revealed in the Bible is subordinated to the "true" God of Greek thought. Sanders, "Historical Considerations"; in Pinnock, *The Openness of God,* 70. . . . we should not be surprised to find that "natural" evil has frequently been explained as fulfilling a higher divine purpose. This perspective . . . found its way into the Christian tradition through Augustine. [Plotinus, *Enneads* 3.2.11.17.] Boyd, *Satan and the Problem of Evil,* 248. Plotinus attempts to deal with this dilemma by positing three Hypostases in God. The first, the One, is indescribable, even by the most general concept of "being." It gives rise by emanation to the second, the Intellect, which "in its totality is made up of the Forms" (*Ennead*, V, 9, 8). . . . Ward, *Rational Theology and the Creativity of God,* 59.

Historical Understandings of Ultimate Reality and God

	Church Fathers	
	Quotes from Orthodox Theologians	**Quotes from Openness Theologians**
Justin Martyr	The influence of Greek thought misled certain medieval Christian thinkers in formulating their doctrine of biblical Logos. Nonetheless even Justin Martyr, who mistakenly held that as a personal being Christ is not eternal but rather was created in time by an act of the Father's will, identified the Logos with Christ, and taught that the substance of the Logos (the reason of God) is eternal. Henry, *God, Revelation and Authority,* V.1.338. Justin Martyr calls God inexpressible, immovable, nameless. The words Father, God, Lord, are not real names "but appellations drawn from his good deeds and functions." [Citing Bavinck.] Frame, *The Doctrine of God,* 109. There can be no question that the Apologists desired to be true to Scripture. Unfortunately, in their effort to make the Christian faith acceptable to the cultured pagan, they represented their doctrine of God too largely in Platonic terms. . . . They drew no clear distinction, moreover, between what people know of God on the basis of natural revelation and what they can only know of him by special revelation. Justin, for example, asserted that certain Greek philosophers (Socrates, Heraclitus) were Christians in that they lived according to the Logos. Reymond, *A New Systematic Theology of the Christian Faith,* 587. [God's] foreknowledge does not imply direct influence or omnicausality or absolute determination, but merely knowing what other wills are by the divine permission doing. [Justin Martyr, *First Apol*ogy XLV-LIII, *ANF* I, 178–80.] Oden, *The Living God,* 72.	According to second-century writer Justin Martyr, God is unchangeable, eternal, incomprehensible, impassible, noncorporeal and anonymous. . . . But Justin is careful not to allow these ideas to totally overthrow the biblical portrait of God as patient, compassionate and loving. He rejects the Epicurean notion that the gods do not concern themselves with human affairs when he declares that though there are no passions in God, he does care for us: God, after all, is "not a stone." [Justin Martyr *First Apology,* 28.] Sanders, *The God Who Risks,* 142. [Justin Martyr] argues for a libertarian definition of freedom as the mark God bestowed on humanity that distinguishes them from the rest of creation and by which God can hold humans morally accountable for their choices. . . . [Exhaustive divine foreknowledge] does not, he believes, lead to determinism because God only foresees the free choices of individuals and bases his election on their choices. . . . In this respect God's decisions are in some sense dependent on human choices. Consequently, God is "responsive" for Justin. Sanders, *The God Who Risks,* 142. Only the proponents of theological determinism consistently ruled out any place for divine conditionality and risk taking. . . . Certain luminaries in the Western tradition, such as Justin, Wesley and Barth, made room for give-and-take relations between God and his creatures. Sanders, *The God Who Risks,* 165. While the postapostolic fathers unequivocally affirmed that God is sovereign over the world, they also believed that his providential control was mediated by angels who possessed free will. Justin Martyr [held this] prevailing view. . . . Boyd, *Satan and the Problem of Evil,* 39.

Historical Understandings of Ultimate Reality and God

	Church Fathers	
	Quotes from Orthodox Theologians	**Quotes from Openness Theologians**
Irenaeus	. . . Irenaeus presents the false and partly gnostic antithesis between the Father: hidden, invisible, unknowable; and the Son, who revealed him. [Herman Bavinck citing Irenaeus in his *The Doctrine of God,* 21.] Frame, *The Doctrine of God,* 109. For Irenaeus, in himself God is the Father of everything, but he contains in himself his Word and his Wisdom. Hence, Son and Spirit are eternal, as is God, but it is only in the process of God's self-disclosure in creating . . . that God extrapolates or manifests the Son and Spirit. [Citing J. N. D. Kelly, *Early Christian Doctrines* (New York: Harper and Row, 1978), 104–5.] . . . Since the "ordering of things" that we know of in regard to God is his work in the world, the notion of the "economic Trinity" is often used to refer to the actions or works of God in our world. . . . Feinberg, *No One Like Him,* 473. [For Irenaeus] Choice is definitive of personal existence. What makes us persons is that we know ourselves to be able to act in this rather than that way. Human freedom shares in divine freedom, yet within the limits of finitude. . . . Scripture frequently attests to the derived character of human freedom, derived, that is, from God's own freedom. [Citing Irenaeus, *Against Heresies* III.17.1–2, *ANF* I, pp. 444–45.] Oden, *The Living God,* 91–92.	For Irenaeus, God's providential will is unequivocally and unambiguously good. There is no "mystery" as to how God's goodness might lie behind children being buried in mudslides or kidnapped. In his view, this goodness is reflected in the fact that God gave humans and angels the gift of freedom. But for Irenaeus this bestowal involves an element of risk. It means that "rational beings" have the capacity either to go along with God's providential design or not. For Irenaeus, this risk did not in any way compromise God's sovereignty, for neither Irenaeus nor any other pre-Augustinian theologian defined God's sovereignty merely in terms of control. Boyd, *Satan and the Problem of Evil,* 42–43. [Irenaeus] rejects the Neoplatonic need for intermediaries between God and creatures: God can deal directly with his creation. . . . Regarding the divine-human encounter he affirms libertarian human freedom and rejects any predetermination on God's part concerning human decisions. . . . Though he does not want to allow what he deems negative passions in God, Irenaeus believes God gets involved personally with us. Sanders, *The God Who Risks,* 143.

Historical Understandings of Ultimate Reality and God

	Church Fathers	
	Quotes from Orthodox Theologians	**Quotes from Openness Theologians**
Tertullian	For Tertullian, the one God is the Triune God a "Trinity." But it appears that for him the Logos was originally *impersonal* reason in God, for he had a beginning. . . . But having been begotten by God with a view to the creation of the world and proceeding from him, he is both a real substance . . . and a distinct person. . . . Reymond, *A New Systematic Theology of the Christian Faith,* 592. What, then, should we say about God as a person? . . . Tertullian was important for the early Christian development of [the concept of personhood]. Tertullian defined a person as a being who speaks and acts. Feinberg, *No One Like Him,* 226–27. Do [Scriptures that speak of God repenting] imply a fundamental change in the divine being or essence, or in the divine plan? No. The Scriptures employ anthropomorphic metaphors and analogies to speak of God's free responsiveness to human needs amid changing historical circumstances. They represent God in human terms as responsively dealing with new human contingencies by taking ever-new initiatives and thereby relinquishing older ones to which there had been inadequate human response. But such passages never imply that something has changed in the essential being of God or that any divine attributes have mutated. [Citing Tertullian, *Against Marcion* II.24, *ANF* III, p. 315.] Oden, *The Living God,* 112–13.	Tertullian sought to do away with all attempts at combining Christianity with various philosophies. . . . He affirmed that God can change his mind. . . . [Tertullian, *Against Marcion,* 2.24.] He sought to break free of the limitations of the doctrines of immutability and impassibility to more easily allow for a reading of the biblical text that affirms divine *responsiveness* to changes in the world. . . . Moreover, [Tertullian] is willing to speak of the "crucified God" who suffered on our behalf. [Tertullian, *On the Flesh of Christ,* 5.] God, he says, is not in control of everything that happens because he has chosen to grant humans free will. . . . Sanders, *The God Who Risks,* 143. To [Tertullian's] credit he affirmed that God can change his mind, clearly seen in God's repentance of his intention to destroy Nineveh. [Tertullian, *Against Marcion,* 2.24.] He sought to break free of the limitations of the doctrines of immutability and impassibility and allow for a reading of the biblical text that affirmed divine responsiveness to changes in the world. [See Joseph Hallman, *The Descent of God* (Minneapolis: Fortress, 1991), 51–66, and Robert W. Jenson, *The Triune Identity* (Philadelphia: Fortress, 1982), 70–74.] God's will can change in response to human decisions. Sanders, "Historical Considerations"; in Pinnock, *The Openness of God,* 74. Tertullian, who could be zealous in rejecting Greek ideas that he found incompatible with the biblical faith, failed to free himself from the Greek concept of static perfection. Although Tertullian often defined God's eternity as everlasting not timeless, and saw that divine repentance implied God changing a prior purpose, he also insisted on the Greek view that there was no change or temporality in God. Pinnock, *Most Moved Mover,* 73.

Historical Understandings of Ultimate Reality and God

	Church Fathers	
	Quotes from Orthodox Theologians	**Quotes from Openness Theologians**
Origen	While more critical of Platonic thought than were Justin or Clement, Origen (c. 184–254) nonetheless synthesized Platonic and Christian principles into a philosophical theology that exerted continuing influence. . . . Henry, *God, Revelation and Authority*, V.1:85. Origen was committed to middle Platonism . . . God the Father is at the top of Origen's system, and he transcends all being. However, since God is perfectly good and powerful, there must always have been objects on which he could display those attributes. As a result, he brought into existence a set of spiritual beings or souls that are coeternal with himself. To mediate between himself and these souls and to mediate between himself as atemporal and the world as temporal, the Father begets the Son in an eternal act. Feinberg, *No One Like Him,* 476. Origen's debate with Celsus was the prototype of [arguments about divine foreknowledge and human freedom]. It grew out of an exegetical issue: Did Judas freely commit his traitorous deed, or . . . must God be held responsible, since God foreknew it? Celsus argued the latter. Origen argued both that Judas willed it and that God foreknew it. . . . Such was the foolishness of saying that in whatever God foreknows there is no freedom, thought Origen, for it is precisely the acts of free will that God foreknows. Oden, *The Living God,* 73–74. The divine constancy does not imply immobility or lack of empathy. The celebration of divine reliability is a religious affirmation that no change can or will take place in the divine nature. . . . But that does not imply that God cannot relate to changing human circumstances. And that God is capable of responsive interaction in the divine-human encounter does not imply changes in the essential nature or intention or will of God. "For, continuing unchangeable in His essence, He condescends to human affairs by the economy of His Providence" (Origen, *Against Celsus* IV.14, *ANF* IV, 502.) Oden, *The Living God,* 111.	Origen stepped up the tension between the biblical language about God and the Greek philosophical notions of God. Origen believes that God is impassible, immutable, uncreated, simple, all-powerful and all-knowing. He holds that because God has foreknowledge of the free choices humans will make, God has providentially prearranged his responses. Via foreknowledge, God atemporally acquires the knowledge of what creatures will do in the future. Sanders, *The God Who Risks,* 143. For Origen and the fathers before him, foreknowledge does not preclude conditionally in God. . . . He rejects predetermination of all things, upholds human freedom and insists that prayer is still valuable even though God foreknows our prayers, since God did not foreordain them. [See Origen, *On Prayer,* in *Origen,* trans. Rowan Greer, Classics of Western Spirituality (New York: Paulist, 1979), 90–97.] Sanders, *The God Who Risks,* 143–44. [Origen] stretches the bonds of classical theism when he affirms that God rejoices at human conversion and experiences sorrow for human sin. . . . He even claims that God the Father experiences the human emotions of suffering, pity and love. It seems that Origen desired to defend a genuine relationship between God and humanity, but he found it difficult given the constraints of Hellenic thought. For he goes on to say that God is truly passionless and experiences uninterrupted happiness. All of the scriptural references to the passions of God . . . are anthropomorphisms and cannot be taken literally. [See Origen, *De Principiis* 2.4.4; Origen, *Contra Celsus* 4.37, 72; 6.53.] Sanders, *The God Who Risks,* 144. Though Origen sensed the tension in his thought here, he was unable to resolve it. He claims that God is genuinely responsive to our actions and prayers (God is conditioned by us for some things), but he has difficulty seeing how divine repentance does not detract from the perfection of God. Sanders, *The God Who Risks,* 144.

Historical Understandings of Ultimate Reality and God

	Church Fathers	
	Quotes from Orthodox Theologians	**Quotes from Openness Theologians**
Cappadocian Fathers	To say anything fixed about God we must abandon the notion of God as a center of change. . . . Basil and Gregory of Nyssa [held] that we use not merely different names for God (conceived subjectively) but rather employ different thoughts about him that signify distinctions based upon the divine nature. Henry, *God, Revelation and Authority,* V.1.128. Gregory of Nyssa considered the Trinity a Platonic idea, that is, the three persons are subsumed under the idea of God just as three men are subsumed under the idea of Man. Henry, *God, Revelation and Authority,* V.1.210. Basil may be right in saying that the Creator's power is adequate not only to create this present world, but also to fashion an infinite number of worlds. . . . Henry, *God, Revelation and Authority,* V.1.316. Social Trinitarians cite as their theological mentors, not Augustine, but the Cappadocian fathers—Basil of Caesarea, Gregory Nazianzen, and Gregory of Nyssa. Augustine began with the unity of God and tried to find pluralities within that unity; the Cappadocians, on the other hand, started from the three persons and sought to describe the various kinds of unity among them. Frame, *The Doctrine of God,* 724. It is God's nature to be self-consistent, and thus to act in a way that is congruent with God's essential being and character. . . . [God] is able to effect all things that are consistent with the divine character and with the divine perfections. . . . [Citing Gregory of Nyssa, *Great Catechism*, prologue, *NPNF* 2 V, 473–74.] Oden, *The Living God*, 78. God remains always consistent with his own nature as insurmountably good. . . . [Citing Gregory of Nyssa, *Great Catechism* I, *NPNF* 2 V, 474–76.] Oden, *The Living God,* 111.	. . . The Cappadocian fathers . . . argued against Eunomius, who claimed that God was a simple essence (not composed of any parts) and so the Son and Spirit could not be fully God: God is devoid of internal relations. In response, the Cappadocians claimed that the terms "Father" and "Son" referred to the *relation* between the Father and the Son. In so doing they held that person, not substance, was the ultimate metaphysical category and thus, in opposition to Eunomius, they could claim that God was supremely relational. [Catherine Mowry LaCugna, *God for Us* (New York: HarperCollins, 1991), 14, 63–66.] Sanders, *The God Who Risks,* 145–46. . . . Gregory of Nyssa chastises the Arians for defining God's being as having no beginning (ungenerate) rather than as having no end. He suggests they reverse this since the unending God is Lord over history, which provides genuine hope. [Gregory of Nyssa, *Against Eunomius* 1.42.] In fact, Gregory claims that the Arian's timeless God is inactive, whereas his God keeps things moving. This understanding of God as involved with time and as a relational being (both internally and externally) was a tremendous break with Hellenic thought. Sanders, "Historical Considerations"; in Pinnock, *The Openness of God,* 78. God may, of course, be self-complete and thus wholly unimaginable, as many early Christian fathers agreed. Thus Gregory of Nyssa wrote, "Knowledge of the divine nature is inaccessible . . . to every created intelligence" (*The Life of Moses,* II, 163). And Basil said, "Knowledge of the divine essence consists in the perception of his incomprehensibility" (Letter 234). Ward, *Rational Theology and the Creativity of God,* 137.

Historical Understandings of Ultimate Reality and God

	Church Fathers	
	Quotes from Orthodox Theologians	**Quotes from Openness Theologians**
Lactantius	The divine constancy is often referred to in the Psalms. . . . Creaturely purposes, actions, and intentions have a beginning and an end, but God's character does not change. In dealing flexibly with the changing scenes of history, God remains faithful to his own unchanging will to sustain, love, and redeem creation. . . . [Citing Lactantius, *Div. Inst.* IV.12, *ANF* VII, 110–11.] Oden, *The Living God,* 113.	Lactantius [claimed] that our prayers and worship do make a difference to God and that God's blessedness does not exclude the experiences of joy, benevolence, anger or pity. [See Lactantius, *On the Divine Anger,* 4.] If you remove these from God, he says, you remove any genuine religion and relationship with God. To those who claimed that God is perfectly impassible and at rest, Lactantius replied that to be perfectly at rest is to be dead. [See Lactantius, *On the Divine Anger,* 4.] God is impassible, but in a way befitting the God who enters into personal relations with us. Sanders, *The God Who Risks,* 145. Lactantius, a Latin writer, also criticized the supposed impassibility of God, producing a treatise on God's anger in which he defended the reality of divine emotions. [See J. K. Mozley, *The Impassibility of God* (New York: Cambridge University Press, 1926), 48–52, and Joseph Hallman, *The Descent of God* (Minneapolis: Fortress, 1991), 66–70.] Sanders, "Historical Considerations"; in Pinnock, *The Openness of God,* 76. Lactantius seemed to grasp that the Christian understanding of God's personhood and his relationship with humanity clashes with the Hellenic conception of God's transcendent immutability and impassibility. However, like those before him, he did not hold this insight consistently. Sanders, "Historical Considerations"; in Pinnock, *The Openness of God,* 76.

Historical Understandings of Ultimate Reality and God

	Medieval Theologians	
	Quotes from Orthodox Theologians	**Quotes from Openness Theologians**
Augustine	. . . Reflection on the sovereign character of the good pleasure of God led [Augustine] to see that predestination was in no way dependent on God's foreknowledge of human actions, but was rather the basis of the divine foreknowledge. . . . He also speaks of the reprobate as subjects of predestination, so that there can be no doubt about it that he taught a double predestination. However, he recognized their difference, consisting in this that God did not predestinate unto damnation and the means unto it in the same way as He did to salvation, and that predestination unto life is purely sovereign, while predestination unto eternal death is also judicial and takes account of man's sin. Berkhof, *Systematic Theology,* 109–10. In the long history of Christian thought, the theory most frequently used to reconcile divine foreknowledge and human freedom involves interpreting God's eternal existence as timelessness. This view appears in the writings of such thinkers as Augustine. . . . Because God is outside of time, is timeless, all of God's knowledge occurs in *His* eternal present. There is no future for God; there is no past for God. Everything that belongs to the human past and everything that will happen in the future is, on this view of God, eternally present to God's consciousness. Nash, *The Concept of God,* 52. Augustine argued that if God were temporal, he would increase in knowledge and therefore be less than omniscient. Frame, *The Doctrine of God,* 551. The notion of immutability most frequently held by those committed to divine atemporal eternity is [that God cannot change at all]. . . . This understanding of divine immutability was held by classical theists such as St. Augustine. . . . As Helm explains, immutability in [the sense that God is immutable if nothing about him could change] is the strongest [sense]. . . . It is the sense that Augustine . . . apparently held. Feinberg, *No One Like Him,* 267.	Augustine, accepting the absolutistic view of God, clearly understood the implications of this view of God in explaining the nature of the covenant relationship between God and humanity. Because God is totally unconditioned, he cannot "respond" to a person's faith. God is not dependent on a human decision for the decree of who will or will not be saved. God has always known who would be saved and who would be damned. Furthermore, God does not decide who will be saved based on foreknowledge of future human decisions because God is immutable. Basing election on any sort of human activity would imply conditionality and mutability in God. God is thus the sole cause of salvation and damnation. Sanders, "God as Personal"; in Pinnock, *The Grace of God, the Will of Man,* 171. God simply sees what is going to happen. Such remarks sound as though Augustine agreed with the fathers before him that God's knowledge of what the creatures do is conditioned by the creatures. This would make God in some sense dependent on the world. Elsewhere, however, when discussing the nature of election, he makes clear that there is no conditionality in God. [See Augustine, *Predestination of the Saints; Gift of Perseverance;* and *Enchiridion,* 24–28.] The fathers had taught that God uses his foreknowledge to see who will have faith and then elects those who will. In this respect they thought we had the freedom to become Christians. Augustine, however, rejects such a belief for two reasons: his anthropology and his doctrine of God. The sort of freedom necessary to respond positively to God was lost, he says, in the fall of Adam, so God must choose who will become believers. And if God's predestination for salvation depended on his foreknowledge of who would come to Christ, then God's will would be dependent on humanity, and that would be a violation of the divine immutability and impassibility. God is not dependent in any respect on anything or anyone, however, so the gift of salvation must be totally independent of human agents. Sanders, *The God Who Risks,* 148.

Historical Understandings of Ultimate Reality and God

	Medieval Theologians	
	Quotes from Orthodox Theologians	**Quotes from Openness Theologians**
Augustine	. . . Augustine and others . . . argue that *time is the succession of ideas in a finite mind,* and since God being omniscient can have no such succession in his mind, therefore, he is "timeless," which "timeless eternity" is to be viewed as qualitatively separate and distinct from time. Reymond, *A New Systematic Theology of the Christian Faith,* 173. Many Christian thinkers, for example, Augustine . . . have denied that men have the freedom of indifference, that is, the freedom to choose either of incompatible courses of action with equal ease and out of no necessity, or the freedom to act in a way contrary to their nature. They have, however, acknowledged that men have the freedom of spontaneity, that is, that men normally can choose and act as they want *(lubentia rationalis),* which means that as long as their acts are expressions of what they want to do, then their acts are to be viewed as free even if what they will is in some way determined. Reymond, *A New Systematic Theology of the Christian Faith,* 191. God cooperates so as to allow the *effects* of our freedom but not to applaud its *de*fects. God allows freedom to be penultimately *effective,* even permitting freedom to distort an otherwise good creation, but that does not mean that God affirms . . . the *de*fective side of freedom. [Augustine, *Against Two Letters of the Pelagians* I, *NPNF* 1 III, 377–90.] . . . [An argument for absolute divine omnicausal determination] has not, on the whole, been a characteristic of Christian doctrines of providence, even in traditions that have strongly stressed predestination. Christian doctrines of providence have sought earnestly to preserve the dimension of the free, responsible will that falls and becomes radically self-alienated through sin . . . [Augustine, *Spirit and Letter,* chaps. 52–58, *NPNF* 1 V, 106–9.] Oden, *The Living God,* 284.	Augustine seems to affirm "specific sovereignty," according to which each and every event that happens is decreed by God to occur. Sanders, *The God Who Risks,* 149. Regarding divine repentance, Augustine is well aware of the numerous biblical texts that speak of God's "changing his mind," but such texts are written for "babes" and do not properly refer to God. [Augustine, *On The Trinity* 1.1.2.] Sanders, *The God Who Risks,* 149. God experiences no emotion of pity or anger despite the fact that his work effects salvation and punishment. [Augustine, *City of God,* 9.5.] The Bible, when speaking of divine wrath, anger, love and mercy, must not be taken literally. Sanders, *The God Who Risks,* 150. Must not God in some sense *become* Lord when he creates? Augustine's reply is that being Lord does not belong to the nature of God; otherwise the creation would have to be eternal. God may be said to "become" Lord, but that is only an "accidental" relation and does not affect the being of God. [Augustine, *On the Trinity* 5.16.17.] Sanders, *The God Who Risks,* 150. Augustine was wrong to have said that God does not grieve over the suffering of the world. . . . Pinnock, *Most Moved Mover,* 27. [The perspective that natural evil fulfills a divine purpose] can be traced back to Platonic and Stoic philosophy, but it found its way into the Christian tradition through Augustine. The essence of Augustine's argument is that since all things occur in accordance with "Divine Providence," everything that happens by "natural" causes . . . must ultimately play a useful role within God's plan. Boyd, *Satan and the Problem of Evil,* 248.

Historical Understandings of Ultimate Reality and God

	Medieval Theologians	
	Quotes from Orthodox Theologians	**Quotes from Openness Theologians**
Anselm	[Anselm] attaches universal philosophic validity to claims made about God on the basis of general divine revelation. Anselm leaves us unsure about the limits of philosophical argumentation, through which he establishes not only God's self-existence, but also the divine attributes of sensibility, omnipotence, compassion, justice and goodness. . . . Henry, *God, Revelation and Authority,* V.1:91. Scripture rarely uses *perfect* as a divine attribute. . . . Whatever may be said about this terminology as such, it is plain that in Scripture every attribute ascribed to God is supremely excellent. . . . So it is right to ascribe to God the highest perfections in all his attributes. The name given to God by Anselm of Canterbury, therefore, is appropriate: God is "a being than which nothing greater can be conceived." [Anselm, *Proslogium,* chap. 2, in *Saint Anselm: Basic Writings,* ed. S. N. Deane (La Salle, IL: Open Court, 1962), 7.] Frame, *The Doctrine of God,* 403–4. . . . The classical God is immutable in the strong sense of the term. This means he is devoid of any change, and in fact cannot change. He is changeless in his being, attributes, will, and purposes, but his knowledge also is unchangeable and he cannot change relationally. . . . Scriptural language suggesting otherwise must be understood anthropomorphically. . . . Impassibility . . . comes along with immutability, for if God cannot change at all, he cannot change emotionally either, and classical theists agree that God cannot become angry, sad, or happy. As Anselm explains in an oft-quoted passage, God as compassionate means we experience things in times of need that suggest God's compassion, but God does not actually feel that emotion or any other. [Anselm, *Proslogium,* chap. 8, 13–14.] Whether or not he is aware of our pain as we suffer, he certainly cannot feel it himself and suffer along with us. Impassibility also means that God cannot be acted upon. Hence, biblical accounts of Moses persuading God to relent from his decision to destroy Israel . . . are anthropomorphic. Feinberg, *No One Like Him,* 64–65.	. . . Anselm was wrong to have said that God does not experience compassion. . . . Pinnock, *Most Moved Mover,* 27. This is the danger . . . in "perfect being" (or Anselmian) theology today that also starts from an intuition of perfection and goes to a discussion of the divine attributes by way of deduction. It says, if an infinitely perfect Being exists, we can conclude, for example, that God is thoroughly benevolent, necessarily existent, and a conscious agent with unlimited knowledge and power, who is the ontologically independent source of everything. While I appreciate the clarity it can introduce into the discussion of God's attributes once they are known, I sense in it a continuation of the human speculation that has led us astray. Pinnock, *Most Moved Mover,* 70. [Anselm] also sees God as self-sufficient. . . . It seems that, in seeking an idea of perfection, one seeks for the highest degree of personal perfections (those that a rational being would find worthy of choice). One then seeks to eliminate from this idea all possible defects which could arise from dependence on other realities. Thus one achieves the idea of a self-existent rational agent. Ward, *Rational Theology and the Creativity of God,* 136. . . . Whereas since Anselm the dominant way of thinking about the atonement focused on what it accomplished for humanity (reconciliation to God). . . . the view I am espousing in this chapter is that . . . Christ's achievement on the cross is first and foremost a cosmic event—it defeats Satan. Boyd, *God at War,* 240–41. Few points in the theistic metaphysic are as clear as that God . . . must, somehow, *transcend* space. . . . This argument . . . is developed with considerable subtlety by Anselm in *Monologium,* chapters 20–24. Hasker, *God, Time, and Knowledge,* 178.

Historical Understandings of Ultimate Reality and God

<table>
<tr><th></th><th colspan="2">Medieval Theologians</th></tr>
<tr><th></th><th>Quotes from Orthodox Theologians</th><th>Quotes from Openness Theologians</th></tr>
<tr><td>Thomas Aquinas</td><td>[The Thomistic] priority for philosophical theology as an indispensable preparation for biblical theology unwittingly encouraged modern philosophers to neglect biblical theology and even to revolt against it.
Henry, God, Revelation and Authority, V.1:89–90.

Some famous theologians and philosophers have been surprisingly ambivalent on the question of the incompatibility of divine foreknowledge and human freedom. Thomas Aquinas writes that . . . "the act of sin not only belongs to the realm of being but is also an act, and from both these points of view it somehow comes from God." [Summa Theologiae 1a 2aer. 79.2.] Yet at the same time Aquinas wishes to deny that God is the author of evil, or, more exactly, to deny that he is the author of sin.
Helm, Eternal God, 144–45.

One final belief of classical theism is . . . [that] God as totally transcendent cannot be completely known by us. We may attribute our characteristics to God, but as Aquinas reminds us, we do so only analogically. . . . This means that in traditional theism there are limits on knowing and naming God.
Feinberg, No One Like Him, 155.

The strong conception of immutability associated with the classical theism of . . . Aquinas says that God is utterly incapable of any change whatsoever. . . . [God] must be absolutely changeless; and if absolutely immutable, he must also be impassible, for change in emotions and being affected by his creatures' thoughts and actions are changes.
Feinberg, No One Like Him, 264.

. . . Thomas felt it necessary to affirm [the] eternity of God. {He taught] not only divine eternity and immutability but also . . . divine simplicity. . . . [For Aquinas] immutability requires timeless eternity.
Feinberg, No One Like Him, 384.</td><td>In his Summa Theologica, Aquinas presents arguments for the existence of God based on the philosophy of Aristotle and concludes at the end of each proof, "This is what everyone calls God." But is it God and ought it to be? Do we really want to assume that God is an unmoved mover or something approximating it? Surely the gospel does not view God in terms of changeless thought and timeless being but in reference to historical events. . . . Because of God's complete actuality of being, God must not be really related to creatures because to be really related would imply a kind of imperfection in God. Even the fact that there are creatures makes no real difference to God. Aquinas allowed natural theology to determine the doctrine of God to some extent.
Pinnock, Most Moved Mover, 70–71.

Aquinas . . . [argued] that what is eternal cannot be contingent, for what is eternal could not have been other than what it is. Hence Aquinas construes God as being in every respect the eternal cause of the temporal, contingent world. . . .
Boyd, Satan and the Problem of Evil, 378.

In the Thomist conception . . . God is said to be absolutely simple. Thus there cannot really be distinct ideas in God; for, if there were, they would be related to each other, but there are no internal relations in a purely simple (non-complex) being. . . . Here, the Platonic strain in Thomas's thought comes to the fore, and dominates his concept of God.
Ward, Rational Theology and the Creativity of God, 54.

It is, perhaps, surprising that [the doctrine of God's infinity] is the one that was baptized into Christian orthodoxy, most notably by Thomas Aquinas. . . . Aristotle's metaphysical arguments from intelligibility to an immutable, eternal prime mover put in classical form the process of thought which still underlies the rational justification of theism.
Ward, Rational Theology and the Creativity of God, 214.</td></tr>
</table>

Historical Understandings of Ultimate Reality and God

	Medieval Theologians	
	Quotes from Orthodox Theologians	**Quotes from Openness Theologians**
Thomas Aquinas	A more serious concern is that these doctrines fall under the scholastic heading of natural reason, which in Aquinas's view is prior to faith. . . . It involves reasoning from God's effects to his nature, without the aid of revelation, and under the assumption that God's effects are better known to us than he is. In other words, Aquinas is recommending autonomous reasoning, which is self-consciously removed from the authority of God's Word, enabling us to argue from the same premises as Plato or Aristotle. Frame, *The Doctrine of God,* 224–25. In order to arrive at a first unmoved mover, Aquinas argues that the series of things moved by other things in motion cannot regress to infinity since such a regress would rule out a first mover. Reymond, *A New Systematic Theology of the Christian Faith,* 135. Thomas Aquinas brilliantly argued that everything temporal tends to change toward better and worse qualities; hence God's will, justice, and holiness do not change toward better and worse, because they are always already insurmountably good. (Aquinas, *Suma Theologica,* I.Q9.I.38.) Oden, *The Living God,* 112.	Thomas Aquinas . . . sought to harmonize the biblical-classical synthesis he inherited from the Christian tradition with the newly discovered works of Aristotle. . . . Aquinas believed that God is pure actuality containing no potentiality. That is, there can be no "becoming" for God because he is eternally actualized. Sanders, *The God Who Risks,* 152. For Aquinas, the creatures' relationship with God is "real," whereas God's relationship to the creation is only "logical." What he meant by this is that the very being of God is not altered by the creation, since God would remain God without a creation. Fair enough, but it seems that when he compares the divine-human relationship to that of a stone-human relationship, it becomes difficult to think of the relationship in personal terms. God, he says, is like a stone column to which we stand in relation. The column may be on our right or our left, but the relation to the column is always in us and not the column. Moreover, his views on predestination make it clear that God does not enter into give-and-take relations with us. Our prayers can never affect God, he says. Rather, God has ordained our prayer as a means of bringing about whatever the divine will has decreed. Sanders, *The God Who Risks,* 152–53. Thomas Aquinas . . . embraced the Boethian doctrine of divine timelessness, and by so doing he contributed greatly to its continued popularity down to the present. . . . By a more penetrating statement of the argument for incompatibilism, he also brought about new insight into the character of the [defense of compatibilism] provided by the doctrine of timelessness. Hasker, *God, Time, and Knowledge,* 8. The belief that God is immutable in this sense . . . came, I suspect, from neo-Platonism. For a Platonist things which change are inferior to things which do not change. Aquinas, claiming that God is altogether unchangeable, gives as one of his reasons that "anything in change acquires something through its change, attaining something not previously attained." [Aquinas, *Summa Theologiae*, ii.Ia.9.I Swinburne, *The Coherence of Theism,* 215.

Historical Understandings of Ultimate Reality and God

	Reformation and Post-Reformation Theologians	
	Quotes from Orthodox Theologians	**Quotes from Openness Theologians**
Martin Luther	Luther uses some very strong expressions respecting our inability to know something of the Being or essence of God. On the one hand he distinguishes between the *Deus absconditus* (hidden God) and the *Deus revelatus* (revealed God); but on the other hand he also asserts that in knowing the *Deus revelatus,* we only know Him in his hiddenness. By this he means that even in His revelation God has not manifested Himself entirely *as He is essentially,* but as to His essence still remains shrouded in impenetrable darkness. We know God only insofar as He enters into relations with us. Berkhof, *Systematic Theology,* 43. Martin Luther accepted this compatibilist approach to human freedom. . . . For Luther . . . "both good men and bad men do what they want: what they lack is the ability to change their desires." [Citing Anthony Kenny, *The God of the Philosophers,* 73.] Nash, *The Concept of God,* 54. Luther . . . contended that Christ's death as a ransom was paid to Satan who then released his hold upon God's elect. Reymond, *A New Systematic Theology of the Christian Faith,* 656. Luther distinguished what he called the *deus absconditus* (the hidden God) from the *deus revelatus* (the revealed God). The latter refers specifically to Jesus Christ, while the former speaks of God as an immaterial being about whom we know very little. Jesus, God's fullest revelation, somewhat shows us what the hidden God is like, but we can never get a precise picture of the hidden God. Feinberg, *No One Like Him,* 60.	Luther's theology of the cross allows him to return to the "fatherhood" of God by which he contrasts the God of the Bible with the God of Greek metaphysics. On the one hand, there is God in himself, the absolute God apart from the world. On the other hand, there is the God of Israel, who reveals himself to us, binds himself to his Word, manifests himself in Jesus and limits himself to our understanding. All this is done *for us,* thus emphasizing God's loving relationship with his creatures. Sanders, *The God Who Risks,* 153. Luther follows Augustine in arguing that God's will is the sole reason for individual salvation for two reasons. First, human wills are so depraved that they cannot choose the good, and thus God must choose for them. Luther thought that humans are still responsible for their actions, however, because he held to a compatibilist, or soft-determinist, definition of freedom. Sanders, *The God Who Risks,* 154. Though Luther often spoke of God's fatherly relationship with us and could, on occasion, speak as though God entered into give-and-take relations with creatures, there remains the other side of his thought, which seems to rule out reciprocal relationships with God. Sanders, *The God Who Risks,* 155. Luther's theology of the cross . . . [emphasizes] God's loving relationship with his creatures. Regarding the two natures of Christ, Luther used the "communication of attributes" in order to say that in Jesus, the divine nature of Christ suffered and even died. Sanders, "Historical Considerations"; in Pinnock, *The Openness of God,* 88. . . . Luther . . . affirmed that evil originated from the freedom of creatures, not from God. . . . Nevertheless [he] also held that there was a transcendent divine purpose behind the creaturely willing that . . . meant that the evil performed by the creature ultimately contributed to some higher good. Boyd, *God at War,* 47–48.

Historical Understandings of Ultimate Reality and God

	Reformation and Post-Reformation Theologians	
	Quotes from Orthodox Theologians	**Quotes from Openness Theologians**
John Calvin	To Calvin, God in the depths of His being is past finding out. "His essence," he says, "is incomprehensible; so that His divinity wholly escapes all human senses." Berkhof, *Systematic Theology,* 29. The Protestant Reformers . . . reject . . . the rationalistic emphasis on the comprehensibility of the divine apart from man's dependence on divine self-revelation. Calvin stresses the futility of speculating about what God is. . . . He repeatedly stresses the centrality of revelation for a proper resolution of theological concerns. Henry, *God, Revelation and Authority,* V.1:134–35. Of course neither Anselm nor Calvin are making the absurd claim that whatever is created has no property in common with the creator. They are saying that there are certain properties which the creator and his creatures do not and cannot have in common. Helm, *Eternal God,* 19. . . . Although Calvin rejects *cause* he affirms *ordination.* God is not the "cause" of sin, but it occurs by his "ordination." . . . In the vocabulary of Calvin and his successors there was a difference between the two terms. . . . It is interesting that Calvin does use *cause,* referring to God's agency in bringing evil about, when he distinguishes between God as the "remote cause" and human agency as the "proximate cause." Arguing that God is not the "author of sin," he says that "the proximate cause is one thing, the remote cause another." [Calvin, *Concerning the Eternal Predestination of God,* 181.] Frame, *The Doctrine of God,* 176.	Calvin says we "ought not imagine any commotion" or change of mind in God. . . . He bases his assertion on the belief that any change in God would be a change for the worse, and this would imply imperfection in the divine being. That is, Calvin does not seem to be following his own sound advice that we allow God to reveal himself to us in Scripture as he really is instead of grounding our knowledge of God on a philosophical principle. Instead, he succumbs to Plato's dictum of perfection: Any sort of change in God would be a change for the worse. Sanders, *The God Who Risks,* 69. Though Calvin speaks of the fatherhood of God in our lives, it is not a Father to whom our concerns, joys and sorrows make a difference. If they did, then God would be affected by us, which would imply some degree of conditionality in God. Sanders, *The God Who Risks,* 157. For Calvin there is a close relation between divine foreknowledge and predestination . . . Calvin rejects the idea that God's election is based on his foreknowledge of merit. Instead, he maintains, it is the other way around: God's foreknowledge is based on election. In other words, God knows all things precisely because he has determined all things. Rice, "Divine Foreknowledge and Free-Will Theism"; in Pinnock, *The Grace of God, the Will of Man,* 122. . . . Calvin was wrong to have said that biblical figures that convey [God's emotions] are mere accommodations to finite understanding. Pinnock, *Most Moved Mover,* 27. [The classical] philosophical and theological tradition, represented . . . with the most logical consistency by Calvin and the Reformed tradition, formally holds that God is among other things altogether above time, change and passivity. . . . Without usually intending to deny free will, this tradition also held that God exercised absolute sovereignty over the world. . . . Boyd, *God at War,* 35.

	Reformation and Post-Reformation Theologians	
	Quotes from Orthodox Theologians	**Quotes from Openness Theologians**
Jacob Arminius	. . . [Arminius'] doctrine of providence—where the contingencies foreknown by God according to his middle knowledge must be understood as genuine contingencies in relation to the will of God—is one of the points where he departs not only from the typical Reformed view but also from his Thomistic models. Muller, *God, Creation, and Providence in the Thought of Jacob Arminius,* 235–36. The relationship established by God with his creatures in the act of creation carries over into the preservation and governance of the created order as described in the doctrine of providence. . . . The doctrine of creation provides Arminius with the foundation on which to construct his conception of the rule and governance of God. God rightly has dominion over all creatures inasmuch as he is the Creator. The nature or character of the divine creative act, moreover, determines and delimits the nature and character of divine dominion. . . . Arminius argues a virtually unlimited rule of God over the creation. . . . Nonetheless, Arminius equally adamantly denies that there can be an arbitrary exercise of absolute power on God's part. Muller, *God, Creation, and Providence in the Thought of Jacob Arminius,* 236–37. . . . The idea that God is independent of all things in that his choices and purposes are independent of influences from anyone and anything other than himself . . . is very close to the notion of God's sovereign will according to which God has the faculty of absolute self-determination. . . . It is by no means clear that more traditional Arminians would find this second aspect of aseity palatable. Undoubtedly, many would object that if God's purposes and choices are determined solely on the basis of his own desires without any consideration of his creatures' wishes and actions . . . there is little room for human or angelic freedom. . . . Other Arminians might contend that God is independent . . . but in order to make room for creaturely freedom has chosen to limit the exercise of that power. Feinberg, *No One Like Him,* 240.	[According to Arminius] God's foreknowledge of what will happen is conditioned by what the creatures freely decide to do, not on God's immutable will. God uses his prevision of who will, through grace, come to Christ as the basis for divine predestination. Consequently, God genuinely *responds* to his creatures. Divine sovereignty grants the creatures genuine freedom. Arminius thus reintroduces into Western theology a degree of conditionality in God that allows God to enter freely into covenantal, reciprocal relations with creatures. Sanders, *The God Who Risks,* 157. Because he affirms creaturely freedom, Arminius insists that both God's knowledge and his will are responsive to creaturely actions. This makes it necessary to attribute different types of knowledge to God. . . . God's knowledge of himself and all possibilities is "absolutely eternal." But his knowledge of beings that will exist is eternal only in duration; in nature it is subsequent to some act of divine will, and, in some cases, even subsequent to some foreseen act of the human will. Rice, "Divine Foreknowledge and Free-Will Theism"; in Pinnock, *The Grace of God, the Will of Man,* 122. . . . Despite their view of freedom, Arminian theologians have on the whole still accepted the classical-philosophical understanding of God's immutability, timelessness, impassibility and so on. These attributes . . . derive more from Hellenistic philosophy than from the Bible, and they render genuine freedom on the part of created beings impossible. Boyd, *God at War,* 49. . . . The original disagreement between Arminius and his Calvinistic contemporaries concerned whether God predestines the elect on the basis of his foreknowledge of their faith, as Arminius held, or foreknows the elect on the basis of his having predestined them. The Arminian position presupposes that God acts responsively to his foreknowledge. Thus, he foreknows who will believe and then predestines them. Boyd, *Satan and the Problem of Evil,* 89.

Historical Understandings of Ultimate Reality and God

	Reformation and Post-Reformation Theologians	
	Quotes from Orthodox Theologians	**Quotes from Openness Theologians**
John Wesley	. . . In the manner of divine providence, though God has sufficient wisdom and power to manage all things well, he cannot deny himself; he cannot contradict his nature; he cannot counteract what he has done or oppose his own work. Wesley, though he recognizes the two aspects of God's character which express themselves as Creator and as Governor, is certain there is no contradiction between them. . . . Therefore, what God has called into existence and has given a nature through the power of his sovereign will must likewise be supported and preserved through the power of his governing providence. God, says Wesley, would like to eradicate sin, to abolish wickedness out of his whole creation, and to suffer no trace of it to remain. But this God cannot do. As a sovereign act of creation he made man in his own image, endowed him with understanding, will, and freedom, or liberty. Therefore, he must respect the creation which he has made. . . . In the Wesleyan conception, creation as the sovereign act of God has prior claim to providence, or the process of divine government. Cannon, *The Theology of John Wesley,* 171–72. [With his free will, man] can oppose God's will and so create numberless irregularities in God's government. Does this mean that God is limited, that his power is not complete, and that his control over his universe is partial? To an extent it does. God has limited himself in the very act of creation. Before things came into existence God was free to create what he would and to endow all things with the natures he wished them to possess. But once God performed the creative act and called things into existence, he obligated himself to respect the creation which he had made and to remain faithful to the works of his own hand. "Therefore, (with reverence be it spoken), the Almighty himself cannot do this thing. He cannot thus contradict himself, or undo what he has done. He cannot destroy out of the soul of man that image of himself wherein he made him: And without doing this he cannot abolish sin and pain out of the world." [Wesley, Sermon LXVII, section 15.] Cannon, *The Theology of John Wesley,* 172.	. . . Wesley was able to develop a truly relational understanding of God and the divine-human relationship as he debated the issue of predestination with Calvinist teachers in the Church of England. Sanders, *The God Who Risks,* 157. [Wesley] thought it reflected badly on the moral and loving nature of God, as taught in Scripture, to unconditionally save some and damn others. Sanders, *The God Who Risks,* 157. In Wesley's thought, the unchangeable holy love of God is the preeminent divine attribute, for only love is given such a regnant place in Scripture (1 Jn 4:8). Sanders, *The God Who Risks,* 158. Wesley's theology was relational: to know God and to be saved meant to be in a loving personal relationship with God and with others. Sanders, *The God Who Risks,* 158. The wisdom of God is displayed in working with humans as personal beings in the divine image, not as senseless stocks and blocks. God enters into genuine reciprocal relations with creatures. In this regard Wesley deliberately returned to the teaching of the fathers prior to Augustine regarding conditional election, according to which God foresees human faith in Christ and elects to save us on that condition. Consequently, some of what God knows and what God wills is conditioned by creatures. [See Sermon 58, "On Predestination," in *Works of John Wesley,* 2:417.] Sanders, *The God Who Risks,* 158. . . . There are things about process theism that I find attractive and convictions that we hold in common. We . . . connect positively to Wesleyan/Arminian traditions. Pinnock, *Most Moved Mover,* 142–43. The method I employ to arrive at . . . the core of the trinitarian warfare worldview is based on Wesley's methodological quadrangle of Scripture, reason, experience and tradition as the criteria for theological truth. Boyd, *Satan and the Problem of Evil,* 20.

PART FIVE

Historical Views on the Attributes of God

Historical Views on the Attributes of God

	Church Fathers
	Simplicity
Justyn Martyr	God alone is unbegotten and incorruptible, and therefore He is God, but all other things after Him are created and corruptible. *Dialogue with Trypho,* 5.
Iranaeus	. . . Who will put up with you who confine the Creator of all things, the Framer and Maker, the Word of God, to figures and numbers . . . and then divide Him into four combinations and thirty characters? *Against Heresies,* chap. 15.
Tertullian	. . . All [the persons of the Godhead] are of One, by unity (that is) of substance; while the mystery of the dispensation is still guarded, which distributes the Unity into a Trinity, placing in their order the three *Persons*—the Father, the Son, and the Holy Ghost: three . . . not in substance, but in form; not in power, but in aspect; yet of one substance. . . . *Against Praxeas,* chap. 2.
Gregory of Nyssa	For who ever said or heard any one else say in the Church of God, that the Father is either separated or divided as regards His essence. . . . We say that it is equally impious and ungodly . . . to think that the Father, in that He is, is separated or split up. . . . *Against Eunomius,* II.5.
Tatian	God is a Spirit, not pervading matter, but the Maker of material spirits, and of the forms that are in matter. . . . God alone is to be feared—He who is not visible to human eyes. . . . He is invisible, impalpable, being Himself the Father of both sensible and invisible things. *Address to the Greeks,* chap. 4.
Hippolytus	For there is one God in whom we must believe, but unoriginated, impassible, immortal, doing all things as He wills, in the way He wills, and when He wills. *Against the Heresy of Noetus,* 8. [God], while existing alone, yet existed in plurality. *Against the Heresy of Noetus,* 10.
Ignatius of Antioch	. . . [God] is above all time, eternal and invisible, yet who became visible for our sakes. *Epistle of Ignatius to Polycarp*, 33.
Clement of Rome	Have we not [all] one God and one Christ? *Epistle to the Corinthians,* 46.
Theophilus	God cannot indeed be seen by human eyes, but is beheld and perceived through His providence and works. *Epistle to Diognetus,* (quoting, with agreement, an unnamed source), 7.
Cyril of Alexandria	God is spirit, and if spirit, not embodied nor in bodily form. *Ad Calosyrius,* 364 A.
Athenagoras	. . . We are not atheists, therefore, seeing that we acknowledge one God, uncreated, eternal, invisible, impassible, incomprehensible, illimitable, who is apprehended by the understanding only and the reason, who is encompassed by light, and beauty, and spirit, and power ineffable. *A Plea for the Christians,* 10.

Historical Views on the Attributes of God

	Church Fathers
	Immutability
Tertullian	. . . The divine repentance takes in all cases a different form from that of man, in that it is never regarded as the result of improvidence or of fickleness, or of any condemnation of a good or an evil work. What, then, will be the mode of God's repentance? . . . It will have no other meaning than a simple change of a prior purpose; and this is admissible without any blame even in a man, much more in God, whose every purpose is faultless. *Against Marcion*, chap. 24.
Gregory of Nyssa	For surely it is not lawful in speaking of the Divine and unimpaired essence to deny that what is excellent always belonged to it. For if He was not always what He now is, He certainly changed either from the better to the worse or from the worse to the better, and of these assertions the impiety is equal either way, whichever statement is made concerning the Divine nature. But in fact the Deity is incapable of change and alteration. *Against Eunomius,* II.2.
Lactantius	The masses believe that Jupiter reigns in heaven. . . . Yet they confess that he was born of Saturn and Rhea. How can he seem a god? . . . The divine command either is always immutable or, if it is mutable (which cannot be), it certainly is always mutable. *Divine Institutes,* 1.11.
Aristides	. . . God is imperishable and unvarying [immutable], and invisible, while yet He sees, and over-rules, and transforms all things. *Apology, ANF,* 4.
Melito of Sardis	[God], I say, really exists, and by His power doth everything subsist. This being is in no sense made, nor did He ever come into being; but He has existed from eternity, and will continue to exist for ever and ever. He changeth not, while everything else changes. *Philosopher, Remains of the Second and Third Century, ANF,* 8.751.
Alexander of Alexandria	Concerning whom we thus believe, even as the Apostolic Church believes, in one Father unbegotten, who has from no one the cause of His Being, who is unchangeable and immutable, who is always the same, and admits of no increase or diminution . . . [the Son] is equally with the Father unchangeable and immutable, wanting in nothing. *Epistles on the Arian Heresy,* 12.
Novatian of Rome	[God never changes] Himself into any forms, lest by change He should appear to be mortal. . . . Thus there is never in Him any accession or increase of any part or honour, lest anything should appear to have ever been wanting to His perfection, nor is any loss sustained in Him, lest a degree of mortality should appear to have been suffered by Him. *Concerning the Trinity, ANF,* 4. . . . What [God] is, He always is; and who He is, He is always Himself; and what character He has, He always has. . . . And therefore He says, "I am God, I change not"; in that, what is not born cannot suffer change, holding His condition always. For whatever it be in Him which constitutes Divinity, must necessarily exist always, maintaining itself by its own powers, so that He should always be God. *Concerning the Trinity, ANF,* 4. . . . If [God] does not contain all that is, whatever it is—seeing that what is found in that whereby it is contained is found to be less than that whereby it is contained—He will cease to be God. Being reduced into the power of another, in whose greatness He, being smaller, shall have been included. And therefore what contained Him would then rather claim to be God. *Concerning the Trinity, ANF,* 4.

Historical Views on the Attributes of God

	Church Fathers
	Impassibility
Justyn Martyr	. . . [To maintain] that [God] is [as unmoved] as stone, and that neither virtue nor vice is a reality . . . this indeed would be the height of blasphemy and injustice. *The First Apology,* chap. 28.
Iranaeus	By their manner of speaking, they ascribe those things which apply to men to the Father of all, . . . they endow Him with human affections and passions. But if they had known the Scriptures, and been taught by the truth, they would have known, beyond doubt, that God is not as men are; and that His thoughts are not like the thoughts of men. For the Father of all is at a vast distance from those affections and passions which operate among men. *Against Heresies,* 2.13.3, *ANF,* 1.374.
Tertullian	. . . The Father was not associated with the suffering with the Son. *The heretics,* indeed, fearing to incur direct blasphemy against the Father, hope to diminish it by this expedient: they grant us so far that the Father and the Son are Two: adding that, since it is the Son indeed who suffers, the Father is only His fellow-sufferer. But how absurd are they in this conceit. . . . Then, again, the Father is as incapable of fellow-suffering as the Son even is of suffering under the conditions of His existence as God. *Against Praxeas* 29, *ANF,* 3.626.
Origen	And now, if, on account of those expressions which occur in the Old Testament, as when God is said to be angry or to repent . . . (our opponents) think that they are furnished with grounds for refuting us, who maintain that God is altogether impassible, and is to be regarded as wholly free from all affections of that kind, we have to show them that similar statements are found even in the parables of the Gospel. . . . But when we read either in the Old Testament or in the New of the anger of God, we do not take such expressions literally . . . that we may think of God as He deserves to be thought of. *De Principiis,* 2.4.4, *ANF,* 4.277.
Clement of Alexandria	. . . Let the specimen suffice to those who have ears. For it is not required to unfold the mystery, but only to indicate what is sufficient for those who are partakers in knowledge to bring it to mind; who also will comprehend how it was said by the Lord, "Be ye perfect as your father, perfectly," by forgiving sins, and forgetting injuries, and living in the habit of passionlessness. *Stromata,* 7.14, *ANF,* 2.549.
Gregory Thaumaturgus	. . . [Normal human passions of grief and distress are not properties] of the immutable Divinity. . . . [The incarnate Word] exhibited in Himself the exercise of the affections and susceptibilities proper to us, having endued Himself with our passibility, even as it is written, that "He hath borne our griefs, and carried our sorrows." *Twelve Topics on the Faith,* 5, *ANF,* 6.11.
Ignatius of Antioch	Weigh carefully the times. Look for Him who is above all time, eternal and invisible, yet who became visible for our sakes; impalpable and impassible, yet who became passible on our account. *Epistle to Polycarp,* 3, *ANF,* 1.99.
Athenagoras	God is uncreated, and impassible, and indivisible. *A Plea for the Christians,* 8, *ANF,* 2.132.
Methodius	. . . With power [Christ] suffered, remaining impassible. *Three Fragments on the Passion of Christ,* 3, *ANF,* 6.400.
Arnobius	God compels no one, terrifies no one with overpowering fear. For our salvation is not necessary to Him, so that He would gain anything or suffer any loss, if He either made us divine, or allowed us to be annihilated and destroyed by corruption. *Seven Books of Arnobius Against the Heathen,* 2.64, sfs 6.458.
Salvian the Presbyter	. . . This does not mean that God is affected by emotion or is subject to any passion. Rather, the Divine Word, to impart more fully to us a true understanding of the Scriptures, speaks "as if" in terms of human emotions. Oden, *Ancient Christian Commentary on Scripture: Old Testament,* 1.127.

Historical Views on the Attributes of God

	Church Fathers
	Eternality
Tertullian	. . . Since this [eternity] is the property of God, it will belong to God alone, whose property it is—of course on this ground, that if it can be ascribed to any other being, it will no longer be the property of God, but will belong, along with Him, to that being also to which it is ascribed. *Against Hermogenes,* 3.
Hillary of Poitiers	His [Christ's] nature forbids us to say that He ever began to be, for His birth lies beyond the beginnings of time. But while we confess Him existent before all ages, we do not hesitate to pronounce Him born in timeless eternity, for we believe His birth, though we know it never had a beginning. *On the Trinity,* 9.57, *NPNF,* 2 9.482. Whatever . . . is created is made in the beginning . . . [but] the Word was what it is, and is not bounded by any time, nor commenced therein, seeing It was not made in the beginning, but was. *On the Trinity,* 100.13, in *NPNF* 2 9.482. But the voice of God, our instruction in true wisdom, speaks what is perfect, and expresses the absolute truth, when it teaches that itself is prior not merely to things of time, but even to things infinite. For when the heaven was being prepared, it was present with God. Is the preparation of the heaven an act of God within time; so that an impulse of thought suddenly surprised His mind, as though it had been previously dull and inert, and after the fashion of men He sought for materials and instruments for fashioning the heaven? Nay, the prophet's conception of the working of God is far different. . . . What then does it mean, that Wisdom begotten of God was present with Him, when He was preparing the heaven? For neither does the creation of heaven consist in a preparation of material, nor does it consist with the nature of God to linger over preliminary thoughts concerning His work. For everything, which there is in created things, was always with God. *On the Trinity,* XII.39.
Clement of Alexandria	It is then now clear to us . . . that the beneficence of God is eternal, and that, from an unbeginning principle, equal natural righteousness reached all . . . never having had a beginning. For God did not make a beginning of being Lord and God, being always what He is. *The Stromata,* 5.14.
Dionysius the Great	Now this word "I am" [in John 8:58] expresses His eternal subsistence. For if He is the reflection of the eternal light, He must also be eternal Himself. . . . God is eternal light, having neither beginning nor end. And along with Him there is the reflection, also without beginning, and everlasting. The Father, then, being eternal, the Son is also eternal, being light of light; and if God is the light, Christ is the reflection. *On John,* 8.
Cyril of Jerusalem	God is Alone, alone unbegotten, without beginning, change, or variation; neither begotten of another, nor having another to succeed Him in His life; who neither began to live in time, nor endeth ever. *Catechetical Lectures,* 2.7, 4.4a.
Ignatius of Antioch	[Jesus Christ existed] before time began, but . . . afterwards became also man, of Mary the virgin. For "the Word was made flesh." Being incorporeal, He was in the body; being impassible, He was in a passible body; being immortal, He was in a mortal body; being life, He became subject to corruption, that He might free our souls from death and corruption. . . . [The Son of God] was begotten before time began, and established all things according to the will of the Father. *To the Ephesians,* 7.
John Chrysostom	But are not made and was, altogether different? For in like manner as the word is, when spoken of man, signifies the present only, but when applied to God, that which always and eternally is; so too was, predicated of our nature, signifies the past, but predicated of God, eternity. Aquinas, *Catena Aurea,* St. John, 7.

Historical Views on the Attributes of God

	Church Fathers
	Omniscience
Justin Martyr	. . . [God] fore-knows that some are to be saved by repentance, some even that are perhaps not yet born. *The First Apology of Justin,* chap. XXVIII. . . . What we say about future events being foretold, we do not say it as if they came about by a fatal necessity; but God foreknowing all that shall be done by all men, and it being His decree that the future actions of men shall all be recompensed according to their several value, He foretells by the Spirit of prophecy. . . . *The First Apology of Justin,* chap. XLIV. And that God the Father of all would bring Christ to heaven after He had raised Him from the dead, and would keep Him there until He has subdued His enemies the devils, and until the number of those who are foreknown by Him as good and virtuous is complete, on whose account He has still delayed the consummation—hear what was said by the prophet David. *The First Apology of Justin,* chap. XLV. And that it was foreknown that these infamous things should be uttered against those who confessed Christ, and that those who slandered Him, and said that it was well to preserve the ancient customs, should be miserable, hear what was briefly said by Isaiah; it is this: "Woe unto them that call sweet bitter, and bitter sweet." *The First Apology of Justin,* chap. XLIX. And when Herod succeeded Archelaus, having received the authority which had been allotted to him, Pilate sent to him by way of compliment Jesus bound; and God foreknowing that this would happen, had thus spoken: "And they brought Him to the Assyrian, a present to the king." *Dialogue of Justin with Trypho a Jew,* chap. XCIII.
Iranaeus	As, therefore, He has promised to give very much to those who do now bring forth fruit, according to the gift of His grace, but not according to the changeableness of "knowledge"; for the Lord remains the same. . . . *Irenaeus Against Heresies,* IV.11.3. I have proved in the third book from the very teaching of the apostles; and that the first testament was not given without reason, or to no purpose . . . inasmuch as man was not yet able to see the things of God through means of immediate vision; and foreshadowed the images of those things which [now actually] exist in the Church, in order that our faith might be firmly established; and contained a prophecy of things to come, in order that man might learn that God has foreknowledge of all things. *Irenaeus Against Heresies,* IV.32.2. If, therefore, in the present time also, God, knowing the number of those who will not believe, since He foreknows all things, has given them over to unbelief. . . . *Irenaeus Against Heresies,* IV.29.2. But God, foreknowing all things, prepared fit habitations for both, kindly conferring that light which they desire on those who seek after the light of incorruption, and resort to it; but for the despisers and mockers who avoid and turn themselves away from this light, and who do, as it were, blind themselves, He has prepared darkness suitable to persons who oppose the light, and He has inflicted an appropriate punishment upon those who try to avoid being subject to Him. *Irenaeus Against Heresies,* IV.39.4.

Historical Views on the Attributes of God

	Church Fathers
	Omniscience
Origen	In Scripture, words like foreknew and predestined do not apply equally to both good and evil. For the careful student of the Bible will realize that these words are used only of the good. . . . When God speaks of evil people, he says that he never knew them. . . . They are not said to be foreknown, not because there is anything which can escape God's knowledge, which is present everywhere and nowhere absent, but because everything which is evil is considered to be unworthy of his knowledge or of his foreknowledge. *Commentary on the Epistle to the Romans,* 4.86, 88, 90 (in Oden, *Ancient Christian Commentary on Scripture: Old Testament,* 6:235).
Tertullian	But what shall I say of His prescience, which has for its witnesses as many prophets as it inspired? After all, what title to prescience do we look for in the Author of the universe, since it was by this very attribute that He foreknew all things when He appointed them their places, and appointed them their places when He foreknew them? *Against Marcion,* 2.5, *ANF,* 3.301.
Lactantius	. . . [Jupiter] did restrain himself from Thetis alone, because there was an oracle that whoever was born of her would be greater than his father. First of all, there was a lack of prudence not in keeping with a god; for, unless Thetis had foretold what things would happen, he himself would not know. If, then, he is not divine in character, he is not even a god. . . . *Divine Institutes,* 1.11. . . . If anyone had discovered something new which would be profitable for human life, he would come there and show it to Jupiter. *Divine Institutes,* 1.11.
Tatian	. . . And I was led to put faith in these [prophecies] by . . . the foreknowledge displayed of future events. *Address to the Greeks,* 29, *ANF,* 2.77.
Cyprian	Nor let any one wonder that we are harassed with constant persecutions, and continually tried with increasing afflictions, when the Lord before predicted that these things would happen in the last times. . . . *Epistle to the People of Thibaris,* chap. 2.
Hippolytus	[God is] fully acquainted with whatever is about to take place, for foreknowledge also is present to Him. *Refutation of All Heresies,* 10.28.
Gregory Thaumaturgus	But as to those everlasting and incorruptible things which God hath firmly established, it is not possible either to take aught from them or to add aught to them. And to men in general, those things, in sooth, are fearful and wonderful; and those things indeed which have been, abide so; and those which are to be, have already been, as regards His foreknowledge. *A Metaphrase of the Book of Ecclesiastes,* chap. 3.

Historical Views on the Attributes of God

	Church Fathers
	Sovereignty
Iranaeus	[God is] the Maker of the universe, the Father, for He exercises a providence over all things and arranges the affairs of our world. *Against Heresies,* 3.25.1. God rules over men and Satan too. In fact, without the will of our Father in heaven not a sparrow falls to the ground. *Against Heresies,* 5.22.2.
Tertullian	Some things seem to indicate the will of God, seeing that they are allowed by Him. However, it does not necessarily follow that everything that is permitted proceeds out of the unqualified and absolute will of Him who permits it. *On Exhortation to Chastity,* 4.3.
Origen	. . . After the resurrection a person will also learn the judgment of the Divine Providence on each individual thing. He will learn that among those events that happen to men, none occur by accident or chance, but in accordance with a plan so carefully considered and so stupendous that it does not overlook even the number of hairs on the heads. . . . I speak not only of the saints, but perhaps of all human beings. A son will learn that the plan of this Providential government extends even to caring for the sale of two sparrows for a denarius. *De Principiis,* 2.11.5. . . . In respect of all these occurrences, every believer should say, "You would have no power at all against me, unless it were given you from above." For notice that the house of Job did not fall upon his sons until the devil has first received power against them. *De Principiis,* 3.2.6
Lactantius	Apart from divine providence and power, nature is absolutely nothing! *Divine Institutes,* 1.91. The Most High Father arranged from the beginning, and ordained all things that were accomplished. . . . All the events that were necessary to carry out the plan of salvation had been orchestrated by God from the beginning—from the first Adam to the last Adam all things were ordained by God. *Divine Institutes,* 4.26.
Cyprian	For, in our temptations, nothing is permitted to do evil unless power is given from Him. *Treatises of Cyprian,* 4.25.
Clement of Alexandria	Nothing happens without the will of the Lord of the universe. It remains to say that such [evil] things happen without the prevention of God. For this alone saves both the providence and the goodness of God. . . . Rather, we must be persuaded that He does not prevent those beings who cause them. Yet, He overrules for good the crimes of His enemies. *Stromata,* 4.12.
Novatian of Rome	We should not think that such an inexhaustible providence of God does not reach to even the very least of things. For the Lord says, "One of two sparrows will not fall without the will of the Father. For even the very hairs of your head are all numbered." . . . His care and providence did not permit even the clothes of the Israelites to [become] "Worn out . . ." Since He embraces all things and contains all things . . . His care consequently extends to all things. *Treatise Concerning the Trinity,* 8.
Polycarp	. . . All the martyrdoms were blessed and noble, and they took place according to the will of God. For it befits those of us who profess greater piety than others to ascribe to God authority over all things. (From an encyclical epistle from the church at Smyrna), *Martyrdom of Polycarp,* 2.1.

Historical Views on the Attributes of God

	Medieval Theologians
	Simplicity
Augustine	. . . Wisdom is equal with the Father . . . therefore also the Holy Spirit is equal; and if equal, equal in all things, on account of the absolute simplicity which is in [God's] substance. *On the Trinity,* 6.5. But if it is asked how [God's] substance is both simple and manifold . . . nothing simple is changeable, but every creature is changeable. *On the Trinity,* 6.6. Since, therefore, the Father alone, or the Son alone, or the Holy Spirit alone, is as great as is the Father and the Son and the Holy Spirit together, in no manner is He to be called threefold. . . . God does not become greater than each of them severally; because that perfectness cannot increase. *On the Trinity,* 6.8. [Nothing] can have existence apart from Him whose existence is simple and indivisible. For, in God, being is not one thing and living another as though He could be and not be living . . . for, in God, to live, to know, to be blessed is one and the same as to be. *City of God,* 8.6. This Trinity is one God. And, although it is a Trinity, it is none the less simple. *City of God,* 11.10. [Even the angels] know this Word and the Father and their Holy Spirit, understanding that this Trinity is indivisible and that each of the Persons is substantial, although there are not three Gods but only one. *City of God,* 11.29. Let it not be supposed that in this Trinity there is any separation in respect of time or place, but that these Three are equal and co-eternal, and absolutely of one nature. *Letters,* 169.2.
Anselm	[The] supreme Nature is in no wise composite, but is supremely simple, supremely immutable. *St. Anselm: Basic Writings,* 76–77. It is evident that this supreme Substance is without beginning and without end; that it has neither past, nor future, nor the temporal, that is, transient present in which we live; since its age, or eternity, which is nothing else than itself, is immutable and without parts. *St. Anselm: Basic Writings,* 83.
Aquinas	. . . In God there is no composition. For any composed thing must have potentiality and act, for without the presence of these, several things cannot become a simple unity. . . . But there is no potentiality in God. And so in Him there is no composition. *Summa of Christian Teaching,* I, 18.
Bernard of Clairvaux	It is plain, therefore, that God loves us, and loves us with all His heart; for the Holy Trinity altogether loves us, if we may venture so to speak of the infinite and incomprehensible Godhead who is essentially one. *On Loving God,* chap. IV.

Historical Views on the Attributes of God

	Medieval Theologians
	Immutability
Augustine	Truth tells me in my inner ear, concerning the very eternity of the Creator, that His substance is in no wise changed by time, nor that His will is separate from His substance? . . . He willeth not one thing now, another anon, but once and for ever He willeth all things that He willeth; not again and again, nor now this, now that; nor willeth afterwards what He willeth not before, nor willeth not what before He willed. . . . Such a will is mutable, and no mutable thing is eternal; but our God is eternal. *Confessions,* 12.15. What then is the same, save that which is? What is that which is? That which is everlasting. . . . Behold The Same: I AM THAT I AM. *Expositions on the Book of Psalms,* 122.5. . . . There is a Good which alone is simple and, therefore, which alone is unchangeable and this is God. . . . This Good has created all goods; but these are not simple and, therefore, they are mutable. *City of God,* 11.1. God's mind does not pass from one thought to another; His vision is utterly unchangeable. Thus, He comprehends all that takes place in time—the not-yet existing future, the existing present, and the no-longer-existing past in an immutable and eternal present. . . . [Neither] is there any then, now, and afterwards in His knowledge, for, unlike ours, it suffers no change with triple time present, past, and future. With Him, there is no change, nor shadow of alteration. *City of God,* 11.21. Thus, there can be no unchangeable good except our one, true, and blessed God. All things which He has made are good because made by Him, but they are subject to change because they were made, not out of Him, but out of nothing. *City of God,* 12.1. . . . What [God] has not made before, He does not now begin to make because He repents of His former repose. . . . In God the former purpose is not altered and obliterated by the subsequent and different purpose, but by one and the same eternal and unchangeable will He effected regarding the things He created. . . . *City of God*, 12.17. . . . No created nature can be immutable. Every such nature is made, indeed, by God, the supreme and immutable Good who made all things. *City of God,* 22.1.
Anselm	[Immutability is the basis for God's eternality] whether God's willing and causing are understood in terms of the immutable present of eternity or in terms of the temporal order. According to the former, nothing is past or future, but everything exists together without any change. *Trinity, Incarnation, and Redemption: Three Philosophical Dialogues,* 159. God's essence is always, in every way, substantially identical with itself; and is never in any way different from itself, even accidentally. *St. Anselm: Basic Writings,* 85.
Aquinas	. . . Anything made through changing or moving must have pre-existed. . . . So God without change produces things when he creates them. *Summa Theologiae,* I.45.3.

Historical Views on the Attributes of God

	Medieval Theologians
	Impassibility
Augustine	The anger of God is not a disturbing emotion of His mind, but a judgment by which punishment is inflicted upon sin. His thought and reconsideration also are the unchangeable reason which changes things; for He does not, like man, repent of anything He has done, because in all matters His decision is as inflexible as His prescience is certain. *City of God,* 15.25. That virtue of the mind which is called Patience, is so great a gift of God, that even in Him who bestoweth the same upon us, that, whereby He waiteth for evil men that they may amend, is set forth by the name of Patience, [or long-suffering]. . . . Although in God there can be no suffering, and "patience" hath its name *a patiendo,* from suffering, yet a patient God we not only faithfully believe, but also wholesomely confess. But the patience of God, of what kind and how great it is, His, Whom we say to be impassible, yet not impatient, nay even most patient, in words to unfold this who can be able? Ineffable is therefore that patience, as is His jealousy, as His wrath, and whatever there is like to these. [For] if we conceive of these as they be in us, in Him are there none. We, namely, can feel none of these without molestation: but be it far from us to surmise that the impassible nature of God is liable to any molestation. But like as He is jealous without any darkening of spirit, wroth without any perturbation, pitiful without any pain, repenteth Him without any wrongness in Him to be set right; so is He patient without aught of passion. *On Patience,* 1.
Anselm	. . . The Divine nature is beyond doubt impassible, and that God cannot at all be brought down from his exaltation, nor toil in anything which he wishes to effect. But we say that the Lord Jesus Christ is very God and very man, one person in two natures, and two natures in one person. . . . When, therefore, we speak of God as enduring any humiliation or infirmity, we do not refer to the majesty of that nature, which cannot suffer; but to the feebleness of the human constitution which he assumed. And so there remains no ground of objection against our faith . . . in this way we intend no debasement of the Divine nature, but we teach that one person is both Divine and human. In the incarnation of God there is no lowering of the Deity; but the nature of man we believe to be exalted. *Cur Deus Homo,* 1.8.
Aquinas	. . . None of our emotions strictly speaking can be in God except joy and love, and yet even these are not in him as they are in us, as passion. *Summa of Christian Teaching,* I, 91. It must, however, be observed that even other emotions, which, by their specific nature, are inapplicable to God, are applied to God in Holy Writ, not indeed properly . . . but metaphorically, on account of a likeness either to effects or to some preceding emotion. *Summa of Christian Teaching,* I, 91. The passions in question are in sinners in one way; in the just, both the perfect and the imperfect, in another way; in Christ as man in another; and in the first man and the blessed in still another. They are not in the angels or in God at all, because in them there is no sense appetite, of which such passions are movements. *On Truth,* 26.8.

Historical Views on the Attributes of God

	Medieval Theologians
	Eternality
Augustine	[A temporal creation] is compatible with the immutability of God's decision. This being so, they should also believe that the world could be made in time without God who made it having to change the eternal decision of His will. *City of God,* 11.4. . . . The world was made not in time but together with time. For, what is made in time is made after one period of time and before another, namely, after a past and before a future time. *City of God,* 11.6. God always is, nor has He been and is not, nor is but has not been, but as He never will not be; so He never was not. *On the Trinity,* 14.15. God does not see things in time . . . that which My Scripture saith, I say; and yet doth that speak in time; but time has no reference to My Word, because My Word existeth in equal eternity with My-self. . . . And so when ye see those things in time, I see them not in time; as when ye speak them in time, I speak them not in time. *Confessions,* 13.29.
Boethius	"The common opinion, according to all men living, is that God is eternal. Let us therefore consider what is eternity. For eternity will, I think, make clear to us at the same time the divine nature and knowledge." Eternity is the simultaneous and complete possession of infinite life. This will appear more clearly if we compare it with temporal things. All that lives under the conditions of time moves through the present from the past to the future; there is nothing set in time which can at one moment grasp the whole space of its lifetime. It cannot yet comprehend to-morrow; yesterday it has already lost. And in this life of to-day your life is no more than a changing, passing moment. . . . What we should rightly call eternal is that which grasps and possesses wholly and simultaneously the fulness of unending life, which lacks naught of the future, and has lost naught of the fleeting past; and such an existence must be ever present in itself to control and aid itself, and also must keep present with itself the infinity of changing time. *Consolation of Philosophy,* Book V.
Anselm	[God] exists before all things and transcends all things. . . . The eternity of God is present as a whole with him: while other things have not yet that part of their eternity which is still to be and have no longer that part which is past. *Basic Writings,* 26. [God] does not exist finitely, at some place or time, [He] must exist everywhere and always, that is, in every place and at every time. *Basic Writings,* 73. . . . It is evident that this supreme Substance is without beginning and without end; that it has neither past, nor future, nor the temporal, that is, transient present in which we live; since its age, or eternity, which is nothing else that itself, is immutable and without parts. *Basic Writings,* 83.
Aquinas	Time is the measure of only those things that are moved; for *time is the measure of motion*. . . . But God is absolutely unmoved. . . . And so we cannot note *before* and *after* in him. . . . He is without beginning and without end, having all his being simultaneously; such is the notion of eternity. *Summa of Christian Teaching,* I, 15. God knows all contingent things not only as they are in their causes, but also as each one of them is actually in itself. And although contingent things become actual successively, nevertheless God knows contingent things not successively, as they are in their own being, as we do, but simulta-neously. The reason is because His knowledge is measured by eternity, as is also His being; and eternity, being simultaneously whole, comprises all time. . . . Hence, all things that are in time are present to God from eternity, not only because He has the essences of things present within Him, as some say, but because His glance is carried from eternity over all things as they are in their presentiality. *Summa Theologiae,* Ia.14.13

Historical Views on the Attributes of God

	Medieval Theologians
	Omniscience
Augustine	. . . We, in order that we may confess the most high and true God Himself, do confess His will, supreme power, and prescience. Neither let us be afraid lest, after all, we do not do by will that which we do by will, because He, whose foreknowledge is infallible, foreknew that we would do it. *City of God*, 5.9. . . . We are by no means under compulsion to abandon free choice in favor of divine foreknowledge, nor need we deny—God forbid!—that God knows the future, as a condition for holding free choice. *City of God,* 5.10. . . . A man does not sin because God foreknew that he would sin. Nay, it cannot be doubted but that it is the man himself who sins when he does sin, because He, whose foreknowledge is infallible, foreknew . . . that the man himself would sin, who if he wills not, sins not. But if he shall not will to sin, even this did God foreknow. *City of God,* 5.10. Neither does His attention pass from thought to thought, for His knowledge embraces everything in a single spiritual contuition. . . . His knowledge of what happens in time, like His movement of what changes in time, is completely independent of time. *City of God,* 11.1. His vision is utterly unchangeable. Thus, He comprehends all that takes place in time—the not-yet existing future, the existing present, and the no-longer-existing past—in an immutable and eternal present. *City of God,* 11.21.
Anselm	[God] foreknows every future event. *Trinity, Incarnation, and Redemption,* 153. For, although He foreknows all future events, nevertheless He does not foreknow every future event as occurring by necessity. . . . He foreknows that some things are going to occur through the free will of rational creatures. *Trinity, Incarnation, and Redemption,* 158. God who knows all truth and only truth, sees all things just as they are—whether they be free or necessary; and, conversely, as He sees them so they are. *Trinity, Incarnation, and Redemption,* 159. . . . The foreknowledge of God is not properly called foreknowledge. For all things are always present to Him, and so He does not have foreknowledge of future things, but knowledge of present things. *Truth, Freedom, and Evil,* 185. If, then, it be said that it was necessary for [Christ] to die of his single choice, because the antecedent faith and prophecy were true, this is no more than saying that it must be because it was to be. . . . But such a necessity as this does not compel a thing to be, but only implies a necessity of its existence. There is an antecedent necessity which is the cause of a thing, and there is also a subsequent necessity arising from the thing itself. . . . Wherever there is an antecedent necessity, there is also a subsequent one; but not vice versa. . . . By this subsequent and imperative necessity, was it necessary (since the belief and prophecy concerning Christ were true, that he would die of his own free will), that it should be so. *Cur Deus Homo,* 18[a].
Aquinas	God knows most perfectly . . . because God is immaterial in the highest degree. . . . It follows that he has knowledge in the highest degree. *Summa Theologica,* I.14.1. . . . Since God possesses no potentiality but is pure actuality, intellect in him and what is known must be utterly identical; hence he never lacks the knowledge-likeness that our intellect does. . . . *Summa of Theologica,* I.14.2.

Historical Views on the Attributes of God

	Medieval Theologians
	Sovereignty
Augustine	We do not deny, of course, an order of causes in which the will of God is all-powerful. On the other hand, we do not give this order the name fate. . . . Our main point is that, from the fact that to God the order of all causes is certain, there is not logical deduction that there is no power in the choice of our will. . . . Our choices fall within the order of the causes which is known for certain to God and is contained in His foreknowledge—for human choices are the causes of human acts. . . . As He is the Creator of all natures, so is He the giver of all powers—though He is not the maker of all choices. Evil choices are not from Him, for they are contrary to the nature which is from Him. *City of God,* 5.9. Our conclusion is that our wills have the power to do all that God wanted them to do and foreknew that they could do. Their power, such as it is, is a real power. *City of God,* 5.9. [God] left no part of this creation without its appropriate peace, for in that last and least of all His living things the entrails are wonderfully ordered—not to mention the beauty of birds' wings, and the flowers of the fields and the leaves of trees. . . . [How] can anyone believe that it was the will of God to exempt from the laws of His providence the rise and fall of political societies? *City of God,* 5.10. We call [God] omnipotent because He does whatever He wills to do and suffers [permits] nothing that He does not will to suffer. He would not, of course, be omnipotent, if he had to suffer anything against His will. *City of God,* 5.10. The sins of men and angels do nothing to impede the great works of the Lord which accomplish His will. For He who by His providence and omnipotence distributes to every one his own portion, is able to make good use not only of the good, but also of the wicked. *City of God,* 14.27.
Anselm	A man cannot will against his will because he cannot will unwillingly to will. For everyone who wills, wills willingly. . . . Although they [Adam and Eve] yielded themselves to sin, they could not abolish in themselves their natural freedom of choice. However, they could so affect their state that they were not able to use that freedom except by a different grace from that which they had before their fall. . . . [For] if temptation can conquer the will, it has the power to conquer it, and conquers the will by its own power. But temptation cannot do this because the will can be overcome only by its own power. . . . I wonder whether even God could remove uprightness from a man's will. Could he? I'll show you that He cannot. *Truth, Freedom, and Evil: Three Philosophical Debates,* 125, 130, 132, 136.
Aquinas	It is necessary to state . . . that everything is subject to divine providence, not only in a general way but even as individuals. . . . Anything in any way existent is necessarily directed by God toward some end. . . . Since the providence of God is no less than the exemplar of the ordering of existents toward an end . . . we must conclude that all beings insofar as they participate in existence must also be within divine providence. *Summa of Theologica* 1.22.2. . . . Things known by God are contingent because of their proximate causes, while the knowledge of God, which is the first cause, is necessary. *Summa Theologica* 1a.4.14. . . . Every inclination of anything, whether natural or voluntary, is nothing but a kind of impression from the first mover: just as the inclination of the arrow toward a fixed point is nothing but an impulse received from the archer. Hence, every agent, whether natural or voluntary, attains to its divinely appointed end, as though through its own accord. For this reason God is said to order all things sweetly. *Summa Theologica* 1.103.8.

Historical Views on the Attributes of God

	Reformation and Post-Reformation Theologians
	Simplicity
Luther	When Christ, the Son of God, was to be conceived in his mother's womb and become incarnate, he certainly had to be already present in essence and in person in the virgin's womb, and had to assume humanity there. For the Godhead is immutable in itself and cannot pass from one place to another as creatures do. *Works,* 37.62. . . . The sacred article of the Holy Trinity teaches us to believe and say that the Father, the Son, and the Holy Spirit are three distinct persons, yet each person is the one God. Here it is said of the one Godhead that it is threefold, being three persons. *Works,* 37.297.
Calvin	God . . . has shown himself with complete clarity in the Father, the Son, and the Spirit. Hence it is quite clear that in God's essence reside three persons in whom one God is known. *Institutes,* 1.16. Therefore, let those who dearly love soberness, and who will be content with the measure of faith, receive in brief form what is useful to know: namely, that, when we profess to believe in one God, under the name of God is understood a single, simple essence, in which we comprehend three persons, or hypostases. *Institutes,* 1.20.
Arminius	Simplicity is a pre-eminent mode of the essence of God, by which he is void of all composition, and of component parts, whether they belong to the senses or to the understanding. He is without composition, because without external cause; and He is without component parts, because without internal cause. The essence of God therefore neither consists of material, integral and quantitive parts, of matter and form, of kind and difference, of subject and accident, nor of form and the thing formed. *Works,* 2.115.
Melanchthon	Now the first article of faith is that there is one unified eternal omnipotent Being, and nevertheless that there are three divine eternal omnipotent persons, eternal Father, eternal Son, and eternal Holy Spirit. . . . *Person* is not a part or a detachable thing, but is instead an essence, a living thing in itself, not the sum of many parts, but a unified and rational thing. . . . *Of the Three Persons, Eternal Father, Eternal Son, and Eternal Holy Spirit, Who are One Unified Divine Being*

Historical Views on the Attributes of God

	Reformation and Post-Reformation Theologians
	Immutability
Luther	[Luther's opponents'] teaching is perilous and perverse so long as they do not teach first of all the beginning and cause of contrition—the immutable truth of God's threatening and promise, to the awakening of faith—so that men may learn to pay more heed to the truth of God. *Works,* 3.178. God is not magnified by us so far as His nature is concerned—He is unchangeable—but He is magnified in our knowledge and experience, when we greatly esteem Him and highly regard Him, especially as to His grace and goodness. *Works,* 3.117. This, therefore, is also essentially necessary and wholesome for Christians to know: that God foreknows nothing by contingency, but that He foresees, purposes, and does all things according to His immutable, eternal, and infallible will. *Bondage of the Will,* 9.
Calvin	Unchangeable, the Word abides everlastingly one and the same with God, and is God himself. *Institutes,* 1.13. . . . No matter how many strong enemies plot to overthrow the church, they do not have sufficient strength to prevail over God's immutable decree by which he appointed his Son eternal King. *Institutes,* 2.15. It is not lawful to inquire further how Christ became our Redeemer and the partaker of our nature. For he who is tickled with desire to know something more, not content with God's unchangeable ordinance, also shows that he is not even content with this very Christ who was given to us as the price of our redemption. *Institutes,* 2.12. When it is narrated of Eli's sons that they did not heed his wholesome admonitions, "for it was the will of the Lord to slay them" [1 Samuel 2:25], it is not denied that their stubbornness arose out of their own wickedness; but at the same time it is noted why they were left in their stubbornness, even though the Lord could have softened their hearts—because his immutable decree had once for all destined them to destruction. *Institutes,* 3.24.
Arminius	[God] is the greatest Being, and the only great One; for he is able to subdue to his sway even nothing itself, that it may become capable of divine good by the communication of himself. . . . The whole of this system of heaven and earth appears scarcely equal to a point "before him, whose center is every where, but whose circumference is no where." He is immutable, always the same, and endureth forever; "his years have no end" (Psalm 102). *Works,* 1.2.43–44.
John Knox	. . . Where [God] says, "I repent," we must understand him to speak after the manner of men, accommodating himself to our understanding. . . . God does not repent. . . . *Works,* III:358.

	Reformation and Post-Reformation Theologians
	Impassibility
Luther	So we Christians must allow the *idiomata* of the two natures of Christ, the persons, equally and totally. As a result, Christ is God and a human being in one person because whatever is said about him as a human being must also be said of him as God, namely, "Christ has died," and, as Christ is God, it follows that "God has died"—not God in isolation *(der abgesonderte Gott),* but God united with humanity. For neither of the statements "Christ is God" and "God has died" are true in the case of God in isolation; both are false, for then God is not a human being. If it seems strange to Nestorius that God should die, he should find it just as strange that God becomes a human being; for by doing so, the immortal God becomes that which must die and suffer, and have all the human *idiomata.* If this was not the case, what kind of human being would God have become united to, if it did not have truly human *idiomata.* It would be a phantom *(gespenst),* as the Manichaeans taught earlier. On the other hand, whatever is said of God must also be attributed to the human being. Thus "God created the world and is almighty," and the human being Christ is God; therefore, the human being Christ created the world and is almighty. The reason for this is that since God and the human being have become one person, this person bears the *idomata* of both natures in consequences.[1] For you must immediately say that the Person [Christ] suffers and dies. Now the Person is true God; therefore it is correctly said: The Son of God suffers. For although the one part (to put it that way), namely, the divinity, does not suffer, yet the Person, who is God, suffers in the other part, namely, in His humanity. *What Luther Says: An Anthology,* 170–71.
Calvin	. . . Though [God] is incapable of every feeling of perturbation, he declares that he is angry with the wicked. Wherefore, as when we hear that God is angry, we ought not to imagine that there is any emotion in him, but ought rather to consider the mode of speech accommodated to our sense, God appearing to us like one inflamed and irritated whenever he exercises Judgment, so we ought not to imagine any thing more under the term repentance than a change of action, men being wont to testify their dissatisfaction by such a change. *Institutes,* 1.17.12–13.
Arminius	. . . Impassibility is a pre-eminent mode of the Essence of God, according to which it is devoid of all suffering or feeling; not only because nothing can act against this Essence, for it is of infinite Being and devoid of an external cause; but likewise because it cannot receive the act of anything, for it is of simple Entity. Therefore, Christ has not suffered according to the Essence of his Deity. *Works,* 2:117. As the essence of God is infinite and most simple, eternal, impassible, unchangeable and incorruptible, we ought likewise to consider His life with these modes of being and life; on which account we attribute to him per se immortality, and a most prompt, powerful, indefatigable and insatiable desire, strength and delight to act and to enjoy, and in action and enjoyment, if it be lawful, thus to express ourselves. *Works,* 2:340.

[1]Luther's efforts to argue against the error of Nestorius has opened him up to the charge that he rejected the impassibility of God. A corrective may be discovered in Luther's subsequent argument

Historical Views on the Attributes of God

	Reformation and Post-Reformation Theologians
	Eternality
Luther	God grasps everything in a moment, the beginning, the middle, and the end of the entire human race and of all time. And what we consider and measure according to the sequence of time as a very long, extended tapeline, He sees in its entirety, as though wound together into a ball. And so both the life and the death of the last and the first human being are no farther apart for Him than a single moment. *What Luther Says: An Anthology,* 542.
Calvin	The idea that God is the soul of the world, though the most tolerable that philosophers have suggested, is absurd; and, therefore, it was of importance to furnish us with a more intimate knowledge in order that we might not wander to and fro in uncertainty. Hence God was pleased that a history of the creation should exist. . . . In that history, the period of time is marked so as to enable the faithful to ascend by an unbroken succession of years to the first origin of their race and of all things. This knowledge is of the highest use not only as an antidote to the monstrous fables which anciently prevailed both in Egypt and the other regions of the world, but also as a means of giving a clearer manifestation of the eternity of God as contrasted with the birth of creation, and thereby inspiring us with higher admiration. *Institutes,* 1.14.1.
Arminius	God does nothing in time which He has not decreed from all eternity to do, this vocation is likewise instituted and administered according to God's eternal decree. . . . So that what man soever is called in time, was from all eternity predestinated to be called, and to be called in that state, time, place, mode, and with that efficacy, in and with which he was predestinated. . . . *Disputation* 16.15.
Martin Bucer	Election, therefore, is the purpose and sure mercy of God from eternity before the creation of the world. . . . [God] assigns them to eternal life out of his patently gratuitious mercy. . . . From eternity [Jesus Christ has been] the destined head of the Church and our reconciler according to God's own eternal and immutable counsel. . . . *Common Places of Martin Bucer,* II.3.

Historical Views on the Attributes of God

	Reformation and Post-Reformation Theologians
	Omniscience
Luther	[God] foreknows nothing contingently. . . . He foresees, purposes, and does all things according to His own immutable, eternal and infallible will. *Bondage of the Will,* 80.
Calvin	God foreknew what the end was to be before He made him, and foreknew so ordained by His decree. Should anyone inveigh against the prescience of God, he does it rashly and unadvisedly. *Institutes,* 3.23.7. When we attribute prescience to God, we mean all things always were, and ever continue, under his eye; that to his knowledge there is no past or future, but all things are present, and indeed so present, that is not merely the idea of them that is before him (as those objects are which we retain in our memory), but that he truly sees and contemplates them as actually under his immediate inspection. This prescience extends to the whole circuit of the world, and to all creatures. *Institutes,* 3.21.5.
Arminius	[God] knows things substantial and accidental of every kind; the actions and passions, the modes and circumstances of all things; external words and deeds, internal thought, deliberations, counsels, and determinations, and the entities of reason, whether complex or simple. All these things, being jointly attributed to the understanding of God, seem to conduce to the conclusion, that God may deservedly be said to know things infinite. *Works,* 2.4.31. The understanding of God is certain, and never can be deceived, so that He certainly and infallibly sees even future contingencies, whether He sees them in their causes or in themselves. . . . But, this certainty rests upon the infinity of the essence of God, by which in a manner the most present He understands all things. *Public Disputations,* 4.26.
Knox	. . . I say to you, that if you imagine in God a prescience and foreknowledge which is idle and separated from his will, that then you fall into the blasphemy of Epicurus: and if you say (as plainly you do) that he foresees things to come which he will not, that then you deny the omnipotence of his power. *Works,* 5.16.133–34.

Historical Views on the Attributes of God

	Reformation and Post-Reformation Theologians
	Sovereignty
Luther	[We may] allow man a "free-will," not in respect of those which are above him, but in respect only of those things which are below him. . . . Although, at the same time, the same "Free-will" is overruled by the Free-will of God alone, just as He pleases; but . . . God-ward, or in things which pertain unto salvation or damnation, he has no "Free-will," but is captive, slave, and servant, either to the will of God, or to the will of Satan. *Bondage of the Will*, 79.
Calvin	. . . God does not indolently contemplate the fortuitous issue of things, as most philosophers vainly talk; but that he determines, at his own will, what shall happen. . . . Wherefore, in predicting events, he does not give a response from the tables of fate, as the poets feign concerning their Apollo, whom they regard as a prophet of events which are not in his own power, but declares that whatever shall happen will be his own work. *Commentary on Genesis*, 658.
Arminius	In his primitive condition as he came out of the hands of his creator, man was endowed with such a portion of knowledge, holiness and power, as enabled him to understand, esteem, consider, will, and to perform THE TRUE GOOD, according to the commandment delivered to him. Yet none of these acts could he do, except through the assistance of Divine Grace. But in his lapsed and sinful state, man is not capable, of and by himself, either to think, to will, or to do that which is really good; but it is necessary for him to be regenerated and renewed in his intellect, affections or will and in all his powers by God in Christ through the Holy Spirit, that he may be qualified rightly to understand, esteem, consider, will, and perform whatever is truly good. When he is made a partaker of this regeneration or renovation, I consider that, since he is delivered from sin, he is capable of thinking, willing and doing that which is good, but yet not without the continued aids of Divine Grace. *Works,* 2.252.
Ulrich Zwingli	. . . We shall see both that Providence must exist and that it cares for and regulates all things. For since it is of the nature of supreme truth to see through all things clearly . . . and since it is of the nature of supreme might to be able to do what it sees, nay, to do all things, and, finally, since it is of the nature of the supreme good, to will by its goodness to do what it clearly sees and can do, it follows that he who can do all things, must provide for all things. *On the Providence of God,* chap. 1.
Theodore Beza	I mean by [providence], not only that unspeakable power, whereby it comes to pass that God has foreseen all things from eternity, and most wisely provided all things that were to be; but primarily I mean by it that eternal decree of the most wise and holy God, from whom anything that has been, has been; and everything that is, is; and everything that will be, will be, according as it was pleasing to him to decree from eternity. *A Little Book of Christian Questions and Responses,* 67.

Historical Views on the Attributes of God

	Puritan Theologians
	Simplicity
Stephen Charnock	God is the most simple being; for that which is first in nature, having nothing beyond it, cannot by any means be thought to be compounded; for whatsoever is so, depends upon the parts whereof it is compounded, and so is not the first being: now God being infinitely simple, hath nothing in Himself which is not Himself, and therefore cannot will any change in Himself, He being His own essence and existence. *The Existence and Attributes of God,* 333.
Jonathan Edwards	The unity of the Godhead will necessarily follow from God's being infinite: for to be infinite is to be all, and it would be a contradiction to suppose two ALLS, because if there be two or more, one alone is not all, but the sum of them put together are all. *Miscellanies,* 697.
Thomas Shepard	God is glorious in his attributes. . . . Which attributes are not qualities in God, but natures. God's wisdom is God himself, and God's power is God himself, etc. Neither are they divers things in God, but they are divers only in regard of our understanding, and in regard of their different effects on different objects. *The Sincere Convert,* I.2.
William Perkins	The nature of God is his most lively and most perfect essence. The perfection of the nature of God is the absolute constitution thereof, whereby it is wholly complete within itself. The perfection of his nature is either simpleness, or the infiniteness thereof. The simpleness of his nature is that by which he is void of all logical relation in arguments. He hath not in him subject or adjunct. Hence it is manifest that to have life and to be life, to be in light and to be light, in God are all one. Neither is God subject to generality or speciality, whole or parts, matter or that which is made of matter, for so there should be in God divers things, and one more perfect than another. Therefore, whatsoever is in God is his essence, and all that he is, he is by essence. *Theological Writings,* 177.
Richard Baxter	. . . [God] is simple, and not material or compounded as bodies are. . . . As simplicity signifieth unity, in opposition to multiplicity, we have spoken of it before. As it is opposite to all materiality, mixture, or composition, we are now to speak of it. *The Divine Life: Of the Knowledge of God,* chap. VI.

Historical Views on the Attributes of God

	Puritan Theologians
	Immutability
Edwards	[If libertarian freedom exists then] He must be continually putting his system to rights, as it gets out of order, through the contingence of the actions of moral agents: he must be a being, who, instead of being absolutely immutable, must necessarily be the subject of infinitely the most numerous acts of repentance and changes of intention, of any being whatsoever; for this plain reason, that his vastly extensive charge comprehends an infinitely greater number of those things which are to him contingent and uncertain. . . . He must have little else to do but to mend broken titles as well as he can, and be rectifying his disjointed frame, and disordered movements, in the best manner the case will allow. *Freedom of the Will,* 2.11.4.111.
Charnock	Unchangeableness doth necessarily pertain to the nature of God. It is of the same necessity with the rectitude of his nature; he can no more be changeable in his essence than he can be unrighteous in his actions. God is a necessary Being; he is necessarily what he is, and, therefore, is unchangeably what he is. Mutability belongs to contingency. If any perfection of his nature could be separated from him, he would cease to be God. *The Existence and Attributes of God,* VI.318–19.
Perkins	. . . It is manifest that the nature of God is immutable and spiritual. God's immutability of nature is that by which he is void of all composition, division and change. Where it is said that God repenteth, the meaning is that God changeth the action, as men do that repent: therefore repentance signifieth not any mutation in God, but in his actions and such things as are made and changed by him. *Theological Writings,* 178.
Baxter	The immortality, incorruptibility, and immutability of God, must, 1. Teach the soul to rise up from these mortal, corruptible, mutable things, and to fix upon that God who is the immortal, incorruptible portion of his saints. *The Divine Life: On the Knowledge of God,* chap. VI.
John Owen	On whom he fixes his love, it is immutable; it does not grow to eternity, it is not diminished at any time. It is an eternal love, that had no beginning, that shall have no ending; that cannot be heightened by any act of ours, that cannot be lessened by any thing in us. I say, in itself it is thus; otherwise, in a twofold regard, it may admit of change. . . . *Of Communion with God the Father, Son, and Holy Ghost*, 1.3.
Thomas Boston	[God's decrees] *are unchangeable*. They are the unalterable laws of heaven. God's decrees are constant; and he by no means alters his purpose, as men do. Psalm 33:11, "The counsel of the Lord stands forever, The plans of His heart to all generations." Hence they are compared to mountains of brass, Zech. 6:1. As nothing can escape his first view, so nothing can be added to his knowledge. Hence Balaam said, "God is not a man, that He should lie, Nor a son of man, that He should repent. Has He said, and will He not do it? Or has He spoken, and will He not make it good?" Num. 23:19. The decree of election is irreversible: "The solid foundation of God stands, having this seal: "The Lord knows those who are His," 2 Tim 2:19. *The Properties of God's Decrees Explained,* section 4.

Historical Views on the Attributes of God

	Puritan Theologians
	Impassibility
Charnock	God is not changed, when of loving to any creatures he becomes angry with them, or of angry he becomes appeased. . . . God always acts according to the immutable nature of his holiness, and can no more change in his affections to good and evil, than he can in his essence. *The Existence and Attributes of God,* VI.345.
Edwards	. . . There proceeds a most pure act, and an infinitely holy and sweet energy arises between the Father and the Son: for their love and joy is mutual, in mutually loving and delighting in each other. . . . This is the eternal and most perfect and essential act of the divine nature . . . The Deity becomes all act; the divine essence itself flows out and is as it were breathed forth in love and joy. "Discourse on the Trinity"; in *Works of Jonathan Edwards: Writings on the Trinity, Grace, and Faith,* 121.
Thomas Goodwin	. . . The immediate cause inflicting [God's punishment is] a "fiery indignation devouring the adversaries." Indignation or wrath is of some intelligent nature provoked. And whom should this refer to? or whose indignation can it be supposed but of this God, "who himself" . . . "hath said, Vengeance is mine, saith the Lord"? *An Unregenerate Man's Guiltiness Before God: In Respect of Sin and Punishment,* XIII.II.
Richard Sibbes	. . . In regard of [God's] tender care over his children, they are as the apple of his eye; and as they are very near, so they are very dear to him. They cost him dear; they are his jewels, and he gave a *Jewel* of infinite price for them. He is interested in their quarrels, and they in his. If they be in any misery, God's bowels yearn for them . . . God's eye is upon them for good. "The Saint's Safety in Evil Times"; in *Works,* 302–33.
Owen	Anger and wrath in God express the effects of justice, and so are not merely free acts of his will. *A Brief Declaration and Vindication of the Doctrine of the Trinity: The Doctrine of the Holy Trinity Explained and Vindicated,* 527. Consider, hence, his eternal, free, unchangeable love. Were the love of Christ unto us but the love of a mere man, though never so excellent, innocent, and glorious, it must have a beginning, it must have an ending, and perhaps be fruitless. The love of Christ in his human nature towards his is exceeding, intense, tender, precious, compassionate, abundantly heightened by a sense of our miseries, feeling of our wants, experience of our temptations; all flowing from that rich stock of grace, pity, and compassion, which, on purpose for our good and supply, was bestowed on him: but yet this love, as such, cannot be infinite nor eternal, nor from itself absolutely unchangeable. Were it no more, though not to be paralleled nor fathomed yet our Savior could not say of it, as he does, "As the Father has loved me, so have I loved you," John 15:9. His love could not be compared with and squalled unto the divine love of the Father, in those properties of eternity, fruitfulness, and unchangeableness, which are the chief anchors of the soul, rolling itself on the bosom of Christ. *Of Communion with God the Father, Son, and Holy Ghost,* 2.3.1.

Historical Views on the Attributes of God

	Puritan Theologians
	Eternality
Charnock	[God] was before the world, yet he neither began nor ends; he is not a temporary, but an eternal God . . . the eternity of God be one permanent state, without succession . . . *The Existence and Attributes of God,* 278.
Edwards	Eternity, that God inhabits, is . . . something infinitely before and infinitely above the whole creation, even above the highest heavens, the high and holy place. . . . It is the eternal state of his own infinite glory and blessedness, in which the persons of the Trinty dwell together, infinitely above heaven and in which they ever did dwell. *Miscellanies,* 952 n.
Shepard	He is an eternal God, without beginning or end of being. *The Sincere Convert,* I.2.
Perkins	God's eternity is that by which he is without beginning and ending. *Theological Writings,* 178.
Baxter	The eternity of God is the next attribute to be known. . . . This also showeth us that God is incomprehensible; for man cannot comprehend eternity. When we go about to think of that which hath no beginning or end, it is to our mind, as a place a thousand miles off is to our eye; even beyond our reach: we cannot say there is no such place, yea, we know there is, but we cannot see it; so we know there is an Eternal Being. . . . *The Divine Life: On the Knowledge of God,* chap. V.
Owen	"But thou art the same, and thy years shall not fail?" If these words are spoken of Christ, it is evident that all the foregoing must be so also; for his enduring the same, and the not failing of his years, — that is, his eternity, — is opposed to the creation and temporary duration of the world. If they say that they belong unto the Father primarily, but are attributed unto Christ, as that of changing or abolishing the world, because the Father doth it by him, I desire to know what is the meaning of these words, "Thou art the same by Christ, and thy years fail not by Christ"? Is not the Father eternal but in the man Christ Jesus? *Exposition of Hebrews,* Commentary on 1:11.

Historical Views on the Attributes of God

	Puritan Theologians
	Omniscience
Edwards	[God's exhaustive knowledge is evidence of God's] peculiar glory, greatly distinguishing him from all other beings. *A Careful and Strict Inquiry,* 11.1.4.109. [If God does not foreknow] the future volitions of moral agents, then neither can he certainly foreknow those events which are consequent and dependent on these volitions. *A Careful and Strict Inquiry,* 2.11.96–97.
Charnock	The knowledge of one thing is not in God before another, one act of knowledge doth not forget [forego] another. . . . In the creatures there is such a succession; but there is no such order in God's knowledge, for he knows all those successions by one glance, without any succession of knowledge in himself. *The Existence and Attributes of God,* 223.
Shepard	He is an all-seeing God. He knows what possibly can be or may be known. . . . *The Sincere Convert,* I.2.
Perkins	The wisdom or knowledge of God is that by the which God doth, not by certain notions abstracted from the things themselves, but by his own essence: nor successively and by discourse of reason, but by one eternal and immutable act of understanding, distinctly and perfectly know himself and all other things, though infinite, whether they have been or not. God's wisdom hath these parts: his foreknowledge and his counsel. The foreknowledge of God is that by which he most assuredly foreseeth all things that are to come. This is not properly spoken of God, but by reason of the men to whom things are past or to come. The counsel of God is that by the which he doth most rightly perceive the best reason of all things that are done. *Theological Writings,* 179.
John Gill	. . . [God] foresees and foreknows all things that come to pass in himself, in his own will, and the decrees of it. . . . God's foreknowledge of future events necessarily arises from himself, his will, and the decrees of it, and are strictly, closely, and inseparably connected with them. *The Cause of God and Truth,* VII.I.1.
Baxter	The next attribute that must work upon us, is the infinite wisdom or omniscience of God. . . . The infinite wisdom of God, must resolve you to take him for your principal Teacher, Counsellor, and Director, in all your undertakings. Who would go seek the advice of a fool, when he may have Infallible Wisdom to direct him! . . . Alas, man, thy friend is ignorant, and knows not what is good for himself. Thy flesh is ignorant, and knows not what is good for thy soul. But God knoweth all things. *The Divine Life: On the Knowledge of God,* chap. VIII.
Thomas Hooker	. . . God is infinitely wise and only knows how to deliver his people. . . . The Lord knew what the men of Keilah intended before they showed their malice. . . . *Writings in England and Holland: 1626–1633,* 64.

Historical Views on the Attributes of God

	Puritan Theologians
	Sovereignty
Edwards	I need not run the parallel between this [the river] and the course of God's providence through all the ages, from the beginning to the end of the world, when all things shall have their final issue in God, the infinite, inexhaustible fountain whence all things come at first, as all the rivers come from the sea, and whither they all shall come at last: for of him and to him are all things, and he is the Alpha and Omega, the beginning and the end. *Images of Divine Things,* 1842 ed., 2.79.
Charnock	[God] hath an absolute right over all things within the circuit of heaven and earth; though his throne be in heaven, as the place where his glory is most eminent and visible, his authority most exactly obeyed, yet his kingdom extends itself to the lower parts of the earth. . . . [For] He doth not muffle and cloud up himself in heaven, or confine his sovereignty to that place, his royal power extends to all visible, as well as invisible things: he is proprietor and possessor of all (Deut 10:14). . . . He hath right to dispose of all as he pleases. *The Existence and Attributes of God,* 362.
Perkins	The will of God is that by the which he, both most freely and justly with one act, willeth all things. God willeth that which is good by approving it, that which is evil, inasmuch as it is evil, by disallowing and forsaking it. And yet he voluntarily doth permit evil, because it is good that there should be evil. *Theological Writings*, 179.
Gill	. . . The foreknowledge of God is so far from overthrowing or rendering superfluous the decrees of God, that the decrees of God are the foundation of his foreknowledge of future events. . . . The reason why God decrees this or the other thing, is not because he foreknew they would be, whether he decreed them or not; but he foreknew they would be, because he decreed they should be. *The Cause of God and Truth,* VII.I.1.
Baxter	The next relation to be spoken of, is God's sovereignty: both by creation and redemption he hath the right of governing us as our sovereign King, and we are obliged to be his willing subjects, and as such to obey his holy laws. He is the Lord or Owner of the world; even of brutes as properly as of man: but he is the sovereign King or Governor only of the reasonable creature. . . . The knowledge of God as our sovereign King, must bring the whole man in subjection to him. *The Divine Life: On the Knowledge of God,* chap. XIV.
William Guthrie	The poor distressed people in the gospel did most resolutely cast themselves upon Christ. This resoluteness of spirit is in respect to all difficulties that lie in the way. . . . But, above all, this resoluteness doth proceed from the arm of JEHOVAH, secretly and strongly drawing the sinner towards Christ—"No man can come to Me, except the Father, which hath sent Me, draw him." [John 6:44.] *The Christian's Great Interest,* 137–38.

	Modern Theologians
	Simplicity
L. S. Chafer	By this term [simplicity] it is indicated that the divine Being is uncompounded, incomplex, and indivisible. . . . [God] being the perfect One, is to be worshiped as the finality and infinity of simplicity. *Systematic Theology,* 1:213. When attempting to define simplicity as manifest in God, confusion sometimes arises. (1) Simplicity of Being in God is not a contradiction of the Trinity of Persons in which mode He subsists. The fact of the Trinity does not predicate three Essences; it rather predicates one Essence and the one Essence is *simple* in itself. The whole of the Essence is in each Person. (2) The attributes of God are not detached portions of His Being which when compounded compose God. His Essence is in every attribute and each attribute sets forth some fact related to His uncompounded Essence. *Systematic Theology,* 1:214.
A. A. Hodge	The term simplicity is used, *first,* in opposition to material composition, whether mechanical, organic, or chemical; *second,* in a metaphysical sense in negation of the relation of substance and property, essence and mode. In the first sense of the word human souls are simple, because they are not composed of elements, parts, or organs. In the second sense of the word our souls are complex, since there is in them a distinction between their essence and their properties, and their successive modes or states of existence. As, however, God is infinite, eternal, self-existent from eternity, necessarily the same without succession, theologians have maintained that in him essence, and property, and mode are one. He always is what he is; and his various states of intellection, emotion, and volition are not successive and transient but co-existent and permanent; and he is what he is essentially, and by the same necessity that he exists. Whatever is in God, whether thought, emotion, volition, or act, is God. *Outlines of Theology,* 136.
A. H. Strong	God is not matter. Spirit is not a refined form of matter but an immaterial substance, invisible, uncompounded, indestructible. *Systematic Theology,* 249.
B. B. Warfield	Everywhere and by all it was fully understood that the one God whom Christians worshipped and from whom alone they expected redemption and all that redemption brought with it, included within His undiminished unity the three: God the Father, the Lord Jesus Christ, and the Holy Spirit. . . . *Biblical and Theological Studies: The Biblical Doctrine of the Trinity,* 49.

Historical Views on the Attributes of God

	Modern Theologians
	Immutability
Chafer	As defined by the New Standard Dictionary (1913 ed.), immutability is the state or quality of being that which is "not capable or susceptible of change, either by increase or by decrease, by development or by self-evolution; unchangeable; invariable; permanent; as, God is *immutable.*" In no sphere or relationship is God subject to change. He could not be less than He is, and, since He filleth all things, He could not be more than He is. He could be removed from no place, nor is His knowledge or holiness subject to change. *Systematic Theology,* 1:217.
Hodge	By [God's] immutability we mean that it follows from the infinite perfection of God; that he can not be changed by any thing from without himself; and that he will not change from any principle within himself. That as to his essence, his will, and his states of existence, he is the same from eternity to eternity. Thus he is absolutely immutable in himself. He is also immutable relatively to the creature, insomuch as his knowledge, purpose, and truth . . . can know neither variableness nor shadow of turning. *Outlines of Theology,* 143.
Strong	By [immutability] we mean that the nature, attributes, and will of God are exempt from all change. Reason teaches us that no change is possible in God, whether increase or decrease, progress or deterioration, contraction or development. All change must be to better or to worse. But God is absolute perfection, and no change to better is possible. Change to worse would be equally inconsistent with perfection. No cause for such change exists, either outside of God or in God himself. *Systematic Theology,* 257.
A. W. Pink	[Immutability] is one of the Divine perfections which is not sufficiently pondered. It is one of the excellencies of the Creator which distinguishes Him from all His creatures. God is perpetually the same: subject to no change in His being, attributes, or determinations. Therefore God is compared to a *rock* (Deut 32:4, etc.) which remains immovable, when the entire ocean surrounding it is continually in a fluctuating state; even so, though all creatures are subject to change, God is immutable. Because God has no beginning and no ending, He can know no change. He is everlastingly "the Father of lights, with whom is no variableness, neither shadow of turning" (Jam 1:17). *First,* **GOD IS IMMUTABLE IN HIS ESSENCE.** His nature and being are infinite, and so, subject to no mutations. There never was a time when He was not; there never will come a time when He shall cease to be. God has neither evolved, grown, nor improved. All that He is today, He has ever been, and ever will be. . . . *Secondly,* **GOD IS IMMUTABLE IN HIS ATTRIBUTES.** Whatever the attributes of God were before the universe was called into existence, they are precisely the same now, and will remain so for ever. Necessarily so; for they are the very perfections, the essential qualities of His being. . . . *Thirdly,* **GOD IS IMMUTABLE IN HIS COUNSEL.** His will never varies. Perhaps some are ready to object that we ought to read the following: "And it *repented* the LORD that He had made man" (Gen 6:6). Our first reply is, Then do the Scriptures contradict themselves? No, that cannot be. Numbers 23:19 is plain enough: "God is not a man, that He should lie; neither the son of man, that He should repent." *The Attributes of God,* 38–39.

	Modern Theologians
	Impassibility
Geerhardus Vos	The next group of attributes consists of what may be called the "emotional" or "affectional" dispositions in Jehovah's nature. . . . We are here in a sphere full of anthropomorphism, but this furnishes no excuse for neglecting or glossing over the subject. An anthropomphism is never without an inner core of important truth, which only has to be translated into more theological language, where possible, to enrich our knowledge of God. The prophet Hosea was not unaware of the relativity and limitations of this mode of description, as may be seen from 11:9: "I will not execute the fierceness of mine anger . . . for I am God, and not man, the Holy One in the midst of thee." What other prophets affirm concerning God in terms of will and purpose Hosea expresses in language suffused with emotion. He speaks of the divine resentment of sin as "hating" (9:15). God's intention to punish Israel is "a strong desire." . . . But not only the dangerous, likewise the friendly, benevolent manifestation of Jehovah's nature is expressed, in similar terms . . . the warm, affectionate feeling that should exist between persons bound together in a previous bond of love. . . . The importance of "loving-kindness" is seen in this, that it underlies and enriches and makes more tender other disclosures of the divine affection. . . . *Biblical Theology,* 275–76.
Millard Erickson	. . . It is evident that God looks with disfavor upon sin, indeed, that sin occasions anger or wrath or displeasure within him. . . . We must avoid thinking of God's anger as being excessively emotional. It is not as if he is seething with anger, his temper virtually surging out of control. He is capable of exercising patience and long-suffering, and does so. *Christian Theology,* 605. God's mercy is his tenderhearted, loving compassion for his people. It is his tenderness of heart toward the needy. . . . The attribute of mercy is seen in the pitying concern of Jehovah for the people of Israel who were in bondage to the Egyptians. He heard their cry and knew their sufferings (Exod. 3:7). It is also seen in the compassion which Jesus felt when people suffering from physical ailments came to him (Mark 1:41). Their spiritual condition also moved him (Matt. 9:36). . . . When Jesus saw the crowds were helpless like sheep without a shepherd, he had compassion on them. *Christian Theology,* 295–96.
J. I. Packer	[Impassibility is] not impassivity, unconcern, and impersonal detachment in face of the creation; not insensitivity and indifference to the distresses of a fallen world; not inability or unwillingness to empathize with human pain and grief; but simply that God's experiences do not come upon him as ours come upon us, for his are foreknown, willed and chosen by himself, and are not involuntary surprises forced on him from outside, apart from his own decision, in the way that ours regularly are. "Theism for Our Time," 16.

Historical Views on the Attributes of God

	Modern Theologians
	Eternality
Chafer	By the word *eternity,* the relation which God sustains to duration is denoted. God, being the Author of time, is in no way conditioned by it. He is free to act in relation to time and is equally free to act outside its limitations. . . . Eternity is more properly the designation of eternity as gathered into one conception. It is in this aspect of eternity that God is said to be "the eternal God." He is from everlasting to everlasting. *Systematic Theology,* 1:216.
Hodge	We affirm, first, that as to his existence, he never had any beginning, and never will have any end; second, that as to the mode of his existence, his thoughts, emotions, purposes, and acts are, without succession, one and inseparable, the same forever; third, that he is immutable. We deny, first, that he ever had a beginning or ever will have an end; second, that his states or modes of being occur in succession; third, that his essence, attributes, or purposes will ever change. *Outlines of Theology,* 143.
Strong	By [eternity] we mean that God's nature *(a)* is without beginning or end; *(b)* is free from all succession of time; and *(c)* contains in itself the cause of time. . . . Eternity is infinity in its relation to time. It implies that God's nature is not subject to the law of time. God is not in time. It is more correct to say that time is in God. Although there is logical succession in God's thoughts, there is no chronological succession. *Systematic Theology,* 275–76.
Vos	In popular language, such as the prophets use, eternity can only be expressed in terms of time, although in reality it lies altogether above time. Some have found in Isa. 57:15, the theological conception of eternity as a sphere enveloping God, in the same manner as time is that in which, by reason of the structure of his consciousness, man necessarily dwells. But the words rendered in the English Versions by "that inhabits eternity" are also capable of the rendering, "that sits enthroned forever," which would yield only the ordinary idea of duration without beginning and without end. . . . Inasmuch as Jehovah is the Creator of all things, He must have existed before every creature and be prior to every development in history. *Biblical Theology,* 263.
Erickson	The adjective *eternal* is applied to [God] frequently, implying that there never was a time when he did not exist. Further, we are told that "in the beginning," before anything else came to be, God was already in existence (Gen. 1:1). Thus, he could not have derived his existence from anything else. *Christian Theology,* 271.

Historical Views on the Attributes of God

	Modern Theologians
	Omniscience
Vos	Scripture everywhere teaches the absolute universality of the divine knowledge. In the historical books, although there is no abstract formula, and occasional anthropomorphic references to God's taking knowledge of things occur (Genesis 11:5; 18:21; Deuteronomy 8:3), none the less the principle is everywhere presupposed. . . . The Bible nowhere represents [God] as attaining to knowledge by reasoning, but everywhere as simply knowing. From what has been said about the immanent sources of the divine knowledge, it follows that the latter is not a posteriori derived from its objects, as all human knowledge based on experience is, but is exercised without receptivity or dependence. In knowing, as well as in all other activities of His nature, God is sovereign and self-sufficient. This absolute universality [of God's knowledge] is affirmed with reference to the various categories that comprise within themselves all that is possible or actual. It extends to God's own being, as well as to what exists outside of Him in the created world. God has perfect possession in consciousness of His own being. . . . Next to Himself God knows the world in its totality. This knowledge extends to small as well as to great affairs . . . to the hidden heart and mind of man as well as to that which is open and manifest. . . . It extends to all the divisions of time, the past, present and future alike. . . . It embraces that which is contingent from the human viewpoint as well as that which is certain. . . . *The International Standard Bible Encyclopedia* vol. 4, 1915 ed., 2191.
Chafer	Intellect in man has its corresponding feature in God, but when predicated of God it is properly termed *Omniscience*. Obviously, a vast difference exists between the two. Intellect in man is hardly more than the capacity or readiness to acquire knowledge, which knowledge, when acquired, as compared with omniscience, is even less than elementary, while the understanding of God is all-inclusive and infinite. There are two patent measurements of the divine knowledge: (1) *Omniscience*, which includes all things concerning Himself and all His works; and (2) *Foreknowledge*, which may be restricted to things specifically foreordained. *Systematic Theology,* 1:192. The omniscience of God comprehends all things—things past, things present, and things future, and the possible as well as the actual. *Systematic Theology,* 1:192. The omniscience of God may be studied both in its archetypal and present aspects. His archetypical omniscience relates to that in God which first planned and designed the universe before it was brought into being, or made actual by omnipotent creative power. . . . With the same omniscience or prescience God foreknows the actions of all moral agents. *Systematic Theology,* 1:193.
Strong	God knew free human actions as possible, before he decreed them; he knew them as future, because he decreed them. *Systematic Theology,* 357.
Erickson	God . . . has access to all information. So his judgments are made wisely. He never has to revise his estimation of something because of additional information. He sees all things in their proper perspective. . . . Even though we are not wise enough to see all of the facts, or the results to which our ideas or planned actions may lead, we can trust God to know what is best. *Christian Theology,* 276.

Historical Views on the Attributes of God

	Modern Theologians
	Sovereignty
Strong	Foreknowledge implies fixity, and fixity implies decree. . . . This fixity could have had its ground only in the plan and purpose of God. In fine, if God foresaw the future as certain, it must have been because there was something in himself which made it certain; or, in other words, because he had decreed it. *Systematic Theology,* 356.
Chafer	The sovereignty of God is discerned in the absolute manner in which all things have been assigned their respective places in creation, in appointing to men their day and generation as well as the bounds of their habitation, and in the exercise of saving grace. . . . Because of divine sovereignty, the saving gospel of Christ is, in various Scriptures, presented as something to be *obeyed.* . . . In relation to existing things, God is in absolute authority, which may arise from one or more of certain affiliations. *Systematic Theology,* 222.
Hodge	[The sovereignty of God is] His absolute right to govern and dispose of all his creatures, simply according to his own good pleasure. . . . The sovereignty of God, viewed abstractly as one attribute among many, must of course be conceived of as qualified by all the rest. It can not be otherwise than an infinitely wise, righteous, and merciful sovereignty. But God, viewed concretely as an infinite sovereign, is absolutely unlimited by any thing without himself. *Outlines of Theology,* 162–63.
Warfield	There are no accidents from the point of view of providence. Not even a sparrow falls to the ground without our Father; and the very hairs of our heads are all numbered. . . . His providence is over all; and by his providence he both can and will always present the means where his grace has determined on the end. *Selected Shorter Writings,* I.114.
Vos	. . . "The Kingdom of God" is not [God's] destiny nor His abstract right to rule, His sovereignty; it is the actual realization of His sway. In this sense, and in this sense only, can it "come"; God possesses His sovereignty from the beginning, and that can not "come." . . . This divine supremacy constituting the ideal state of religion branches out in several directions. At first, so long as the thing is considered in the abstract, it can be compared to a bundle of rays of light and action proceeding from and held together by the hand of God. But this is only provisional; the goal is that all these exercises of divine supremacy shall find their unitary organization in one royal establishment. The three principal spheres in which the divine supremacy works toward this end are the sphere of power, the sphere of righteousness and the sphere of blessedness. *Biblical Theology,* 412.
Packer	. . . Divine sovereignty is one of a pair of truths which form an antinomy in biblical thinking. The God of the Bible is both Lord and Lawgiver in His world; He is both man's King and man's Judge. Consequently, if we would be biblical in our outlook, we have to make room in our minds for the thoughts of divine sovereignty and of human responsibility to stand side by side. . . . God is indubitably sovereign over man, for He controls and orders all human deeds, as He controls and orders all else in His universe. *Evangelism and the Sovereignty of God,* 93.

PART SIX

Open Theism Compared with Other Theological Systems

Attributes of God

	Calvinism	Arminianism	Open Theism	Process Theism
Simplicity	By simplicity [is meant] that God is free from any division into parts; he is free from compositeness . . . as immaterial, it is impossible to divide God's being into physical parts, but proponents of divine simplicity mean more than this. They mean that it is impossible altogether to divide God into constituent parts. Thus, we cannot differentiate God's substantiality from his attributes. Nor can we say that God's nature is composed of various attributes. Rather, God's essence *is* his attributes, and those attributes must be identical with one another and with him; otherwise, we could distinguish various parts of God's nature. Feinberg, *No One Like Him,* 325.	Simplicity is a preeminent mode of the Essence of God, by which he is void of all composition, and of component parts whether they belong to the senses or to the understanding. He is without composition, because without external cause; and He is without component parts, because without internal cause. . . . The Essence of God, therefore, neither consists of material, integral and quantitive parts, of matter and form, of kind and difference, of subject and accident, nor of form and the thing formed. . . . God is his own Essence and his own Being, and is the same in that which is, and that by which it is. Arminius, *Public Disputations,* IV.XI.	Of course, the risk model sometimes finds agreement with the intentions and functions rather than the material content of certain theological formulations. For instance, applying terms such as . . . simplicity to God was intended to protect the Christian conception of God from certain impure conceptions inherent in pagan religions. Though this was a noble motive, it did make it difficult to speak of relationality within the Godhead. Sanders, *The God Who Risks,* 165.	It follows—I think follows rigorously—that there must be two really distinct aspects of the divine being, supposing God to exist, both of which cannot be necessary, although one of them may be so. It is this two-aspect doctrine which, as I hope to show, solves the traditional theistic paradoxes. Hartshorne, *The Divine Relativity,* 15.

Open Theism Compared with Other Theological Systems

Attributes of God

	Calvinism	Arminianism	Open Theism	Process Theism
Simplicity	But there is another special mark by which he designates himself, for the purpose of giving a more intimate knowledge of his nature. While he proclaims his unity, he distinctly sets it before us as existing in three persons. These we must hold, unless the bare and empty name of Deity merely is to flutter in our brain without any genuine knowledge. Moreover, lest any one should dream of a threefold God, or think that the simple essence is divided by the three Persons, we must here seek a brief and easy definition which may effectually guard us from error. . . . The essence of God being simple and undivided, and contained in himself entire, in full perfection, without partition or diminution, it is improper, nay, ridiculous, to call it his express image, (*charaktes*.) But because the Father, though distinguished by his own peculiar properties, has expressed himself wholly in the Son, he is said with perfect reason to have rendered his person (*hypostasis*) manifest in him. Calvin, *Institutes,* 1.13.2.	Hence, it follows that [God's] essence is simple and infinite; from this, that it is eternal and immeasurable; and, lastly, that it is unchangeable, impassible and incorruptible, in the manner in which it has been proved by us in our public theses on this subject. Arminius, *Private Disputations,* XV.VII.	The doctrine of divine simplicity, so crucial to the classical understanding of God, has been abandoned by a strong majority of Christian philosophers, though it still has a small band of defenders. Hasker, "A Philosophical Perspective"; in Pinnock, *The Openness of God,* 127.	God's conceptual nature is unchanged, by reason of its final completeness. But his derivative nature is consequent upon the creative advance of the world. Thus, analogously to all actual entities, the nature of God is dipolar. He has a primordial nature and a consequent nature. The consequent nature of God is conscious; and it is the realization of the actual world in the unity of his nature, and through the transformation of his wisdom. The primordial nature is conceptual, the consequent nature is the weaving of God's physical feelings upon his primordial concepts. One side of God's nature is constituted by his conceptual experience. This experience is the primordial fact of the world, limited by no actuality which it presupposes. It is therefore infinite, devoid of all negative prehensions. This side of his nature is free, complete, primordial, eternal, actually deficient, and unconscious. The other side originates with physical experience derived from the temporal world, and then acquires integration with the primordial side. It is determined, incomplete, consequent, "everlasting," fully actual, and conscious. Whitehead, *Process and Reality,* 523–24.

Attributes of God

	Calvinism	Arminianism	Open Theism	Process Theism
Pure Actuality	. . . The notion of God as pure actuality hearkens back to Aristotle. For Aristotle and his followers, every existing thing except God is a combination of actuality and potentiality. Hence, they can and do grow and change. However, Aristotle reasoned that potentiality is an imperfection, for whatever has potentiality is not fully the being it might be. Aristotle and Aquinas both concluded that since God is a perfect being, he must be totally actual with no potentiality to become anything more than he is. Feinberg, *No One Like Him,* 64. Anselm's key insight was that no being could qualify as God if a greater being could be conceived. To say that God is the [greatest conceivable being] means that "God is a being with the greatest possible array of compossible great-making properties." Moreover, a great-making property is "any property, or attribute, or characteristic, or quality which it is intrinsically good to have, any property which endows its bearer with some measure of value, or greatness, or metaphysical stature, regardless of external circumstances." Feinberg, *No One Like Him,* 210.	To the essence of God no attribute can be added, whether distinguished from it in reality, by relation, or by a mere conception of the mind; but only a mode of pre-eminence can be attributed to it, according to which it is understood to comprise within itself and to exceed all the perfections of all things. This mode may be declared in this one expression: "The divine essence is uncaused and without commencement." Arminius, *Private Disputations,* XV.VI. The citation of a few definitions [of God] may be useful. "The first ground of all being; the divine spirit which, unmoved itself, moves all; absolute, efficient principle; absolute notion; absolute end."—*Aristotle.* This definition conforms somewhat to the author's four forms of cause. It contains more truth of a definition than some given by professedly Christian philosophers. Miley, *Systematic Theology,* 1:59.	In a sense God needs our love because he has freely chosen to be a lover and needs us because he has chosen to have reciprocal love, not because it was foisted on him from without. Pinnock, *Most Moved Mover,* 30. . . . God freely chooses to actualize his potential to be the creator of a non-divine world and decides to have a world which would become part of God's own experience. Pinnock, *Most Moved Mover,* 30.	Traditional theism had trouble explaining why there should be a world. The description of deity as *actus purus* meant that God had already (i.e., eternally) actualized all possible values. This was one way of stressing deity's total independence of the world. Process theology does not have this problem. Although the possible values all subsist in God, they subsist as merely *possible* values, not as actualized values. They are possible values for finite realization. They are in God only conceptually, or in the mode of appetition, not physically, or in the mode of enjoyment. Hence, there must be a world of finite actualities, or no values will be enjoyed. Cobb, *Process Theology,* 63. Viewed as primordial, he is the unlimited conceptual realization of the absolute wealth of potentiality. In this aspect, he is not *before* all creation, but *with* all creation. But, as primordial, so far is he from "eminent reality," that in this abstraction he is "deficiently actual"—and this in two ways. His feelings are only conceptual and so lack the fullness of actuality. Secondly, conceptual feelings, apart from complex integration with physical feelings, are devoid of consciousness in their subjective forms. Whitehead, *Process and Reality,* 521.

Open Theism Compared with Other Theological Systems

Attributes of God

	Calvinism	Arminianism	Open Theism	Process Theism
Necessity	The Bible itself, instead of asking whether God is logically necessary, grounds the very necessity even of logic in God's own intellect. Viewing God as ontologically necessary, the Bible thus implies a specific view of logical necessity and of the nature of logic; that is, God is necessary to explain the world—a declaration far different from the speculative question of logical necessity. Henry, *God, Revelation and Authority,* V.1:259. Philosophers and theologians who speak of God as necessary . . . typically mean two things. On the one hand, they mean that any attribute God has in a given possible world is part of his essential nature. He could not be the being he is without those attributes. In addition, to say that God is a necessary being means that he exists in every possible world. Necessary beings depend on nothing for their existence; they neither come into nor go out of existence. Feinberg, *No One Like Him,* 211.	. . . For as the nature of God necessarily exists, so it is necessarily known. . . . Arminius, *Public Disputations,* IV.IV. . . . The existence of contingent beings requires that we admit the existence of some necessary being. If any contingent being whatsoever exists, there then must be some necessary being. Contingent beings evidently exist. Therefore, the unconditionally necessary being must exist as the sufficient explanation of any contingent being. Oden, *The Living God,* 161.	. . . God is necessary and changeless in some respects but free and changing in others. . . . God is necessary and changeless in nature but . . . his nature is that of a temporal and personal agent. Pinnock, *Most Moved Mover,* 85. . . . We can say that God has established necessary truths for us and God abides by them in relating to us. Whether they are necessary for God or not is more than we can say. Sanders, *The God Who Risks,* 321.	It simply cannot be that everything in God is necessary, including his knowledge that this world exists, unless the world is in the same sense necessary and there is no contingency whatever. In that case, necessity contrasts with nothing and says nothing. Hartshorne, *The Divine Relativity,* 14. I am not claiming for God either eminent reality or necessary existence in contrast to contingent existence. Since God does exist, and since he aims at the maximum strength of beauty, he will continue to exist everlastingly. The necessity of his everlasting existence stems from his aim at such existence combined with his power to effect it. But I am more interested in God's power to cause actual occasions to occur than in the "necessity" of his existence. It is no objection to my mind that if that which has the power to give existence requires also that it receive existence, then we are involved in an infinite regress. I assume that we are indeed involved in an endless regress. Cobb, *Process Philosophy and Christian Thought,* 241–42.

Open Theism Compared with Other Theological Systems

Attributes of God

	Calvinism	Arminianism	Open Theism	Process Theism
Infinity	[God] is infinite in his being and perfections. . . . When it is said that God is infinite as to his being, what is meant is, that no limitation can be assigned to his essence. It is often said that our idea of the infinite is merely negative. There is a sense in which this may be true, but there is a sense in which it is not true. It is true that the form of the proposition is negative when we say that no limit can be assigned to . . . the being of God. But it implies the affirmation that the object of which infinity is predicated is illimitable. Hodge, *Systematic Theology,* 1.V.5.A.	If we consider boundless space, or boundless duration, we shrink into nothing before it. But God is not a man. A day, and million of ages, are the same with Him. Therefore, there is the same disproportion between Him and any finite being, as between Him and the creature of a day. Wesley, *The Works of John Wesley,* Sermon LIV, 198.	Donald Bloesch correctly notes that "God is not 'absolute infinity' (as the older theologians understood it) because this would then exclude the possibility of fellowship with God within the structures of finitude." Sanders, *The God Who Risks,* 29. It seems to me that the Bible does not think of God as formless. Rather, it thinks of him as possessing a form that these divine appearances reflect. At the very least, God chooses to share in the human condition, participate in human history; an intensely and remarkably involved participant. Pinnock, *Most Moved Mover,* 34.	The limitation of God is his goodness. He gains his depth of actuality by his harmony of valuation. It is not true that God is in all respects infinite. If He were, He would be evil as well as good. Also this unlimited fusion of evil with good would mean mere nothingness. He is something decided and thereby limited. Whitehead, *Religion in the Making,* 138.

Open Theism Compared with Other Theological Systems

Attributes of God

	Calvinism	Arminianism	Open Theism	Process Theism
Infinity	Although the Hebrew language has no word for infinity, the term infinite occurs in the King James translation of Job 22:5, Psalm 147:5 and Nahum 3:9. Here the translation represents two Hebrew words meaning "very great." . . . The Westminster Shorter Catechism . . . affirms infinity first among the divine perfections: "God is a Spirit, infinite in his being . . . " and so forth. Although some have argued that the confession limits God's infinity to certain expressly stipulated perfections, the statement that God is infinite in being seems to affirm that God is infinite in the totality of his nature and hence in all his perfections. Henry, *God, Revelation and Authority,* V.1:220–21.	Infinity of Being is a preeminent mode of the Essence of God, by which it is devoid of all limitation and boundary. . . . It is not bounded by anything above it, because it has received its being from no one. Nor by anything below it, because the form, which is itself, is not limited to the capacity of any matter whatsoever that may be its recipient. Neither by any thing before it, because it is from nothing efficient: nor after it, because it does not exist for the sake of another end. But, His Essence is terminated inwardly by its own property, according to which it is what it is and nothing else. Yet by this no limits are prescribed to its Infinity; for by the very circumstance, that it is its own being, subsisting through itself, neither received from another nor in another, it is distinguished, from all others, and others are removed from it. Arminius, *Public Disputations,* IV.XII.	The whole notion of limits on the Divine being is often subject to logical confusion; for it may be held that if God is infinite, then he can be limited in no way at all, since any limit makes God finite, or excludes some property from him. . . . In a sense . . . the possession of any such properties makes God finite, in excluding something from his being. . . . One needs to distinguish between the sorts of limits which are necessarily ascribable to God, if he is to be named at all, and the sorts of limits which are removable restrictions on his perfection. Ward, *Rational Theology and the Creativity of God,* 123.	Conceptual experience can be infinite, but it belongs to the nature of physical experience that it is finite. An actual entity in the temporal world is to be conceived as originated by physical experience with its process of completion motivated by consequent, conceptual experience initially derived from God. God is to be conceived as originated by conceptual experience with his process of completion motivated by consequent, physical experience, initially derived from the temporal world. Whitehead, *Process and Reality,* 524.

Open Theism Compared with Other Theological Systems

Attributes of God

	Calvinism	Arminianism	Open Theism	Process Theism
Eternality	To say that God is eternal is . . . to say that he is not in time. There is for him no past and no future. It makes no sense to ask how long God has existed, or to divide up his life into periods of time. He possesses the whole of his life at once: it is not lived successively. Helm, *Eternal God,* 23–24. God is also infinite in relation to time. He is without beginning or end, he is free from all succession of time, and he is the cause of time. That he is without beginning or end may be inferred from the doctrine of his self-existence; he who exists by reason of his nature rather than his volition, must always have existed and must continue to exist forever. That God is eternal is abundantly taught in Scripture. He is called "the Everlasting God. . . ." Thiessen, *Lectures in Systematic Theology,* 78.	Eternity is a pre-eminent mode of the Essence of God, by which it is devoid of time with regard to the term or limits of beginning and end, because it is of infinite being; it is also devoid of time with regard to the succession of former and latter, of past and future, because it is of simple being, which is never in capability, but always in act. . . . According to this mode, therefore, the Being of God is always the universal, the whole, the plentitude of his essence, closely, fixedly, and at every instant present with it, resembling a moment which is also devoid of intelligible parts, and never flows onward progressively, but always continues within itself. Arminius, *Public Disputations,* IV.XIV.	Of course God is "above time," for our concept of time is simply the way we measure change. This doesn't mean, however, that there is no *sequence* in God's experience. A fundamental aspect of classical theological thinking, again revealing the influence of Plato, was that God experiences no "before" or "after." He experiences all of time in a single, changeless, eternal moment. . . . Doesn't every page of the Bible paint a portrait of a God who experiences things, thinks things, and responds to things *sequentially?* Boyd, *God of the Possible,* 131. God's time cannot be the only measurement between God and created objects; it must refer to the everlasting relations of the Trinity as well. Pinnock, *Most Moved Mover,* 99. If God is personal he is temporal, and if he is temporal then he is inside and not outside of time. Time is not a "thing" that God may or may not have created. Time is the concomitant of God and personal life. It exists because of God's nature. Pinnock, *Most Moved Mover,* 98.	The perfection of God's subjective aim, derived from the completeness of his primordial nature, issues into the character of his consequent nature. In it there is no loss, no obstruction. The world is felt in a unison of immediacy. The property of combining creative advance with the retention of mutual immediacy is what in the previous section is meant by the term "everlasting." Whitehead, *Process and Reality,* 524–25.

Open Theism Compared with Other Theological Systems

Attributes of God

	Calvinism	Arminianism	Open Theism	Process Theism
Eternality	The infinity of God in reference to duration is called eternity to which these three things are ascribed: (1) that it is without beginning; (2) without end; (3) without succession. . . . We maintain that God is free from every difference of time, and no less from succession than from beginning and end. Turretin, *Institutes of Elenctic Theology,* 1.3.10.I. The eternity of God cannot have succession because his essence, with which it is really identified, admits none. This is so both because it is perfectly simple and immutable . . . and because it is unmeasurable, as being the first and independent. Turretin, *Institutes of Elenctic Theology,* 1.3.10.V.	. . . God is an eternal Being. "His goings are from everlasting," and will continue to everlasting. As he ever was, so he ever will be; as there was no beginning of his existence, so there will be no end. . . . Perhaps it would be proper to say, "He is from everlasting to everlasting." Wesley, *Compend of Wesley's Theology,* 44. That God is eternal is the constant declaration of Scripture: in fact this is a predicate more habitual than any other, being the first revelation of Himself to His people, I AM THAT I AM. . . . The perfect idea of eternity, as it is in the human mind, cannot tolerate duration or succession of thoughts as necessary to the Divine consciousness. And this is the deep perplexity of our human intellect, which however must accept the profound meaning of the name I AM, as teaching an eternal now enfolding and surrounding the successive existence of time. Pope, *A Compendium of Christian Theology,* 1:296–97.	. . . If God is timeless and incapable of change, how can God be born, grow up, live with and among people, suffer and die, as we believe he did as incarnated in Jesus? Hasker, "A Philosophical Perspective"; in Pinnock, *The Openness of God,* 128–29. There is temporal succession in God's thinking; he remembers the past, interacts with the present and anticipates the future. . . . God is not thought of in terms of timelessness, whatever that means. At least since creation, the divine life has been temporally ordered. . . . How indeed could God be our redeemer if he were timeless? Pinnock, *Most Moved Mover,* 32–33. God is a temporal agent. He is above time in the sense that he is above finite experience and measurement of time but he is not beyond "before and after" or beyond sequence of events. Scripture presents God as temporally everlasting, not timelessly eternal. . . . Clearly God is temporally related to creatures and projects himself and his actions along a temporal path. Pinnock, *Most Moved Mover,* 96–97.	While the new theism does indeed conceive God as both absolute and relative, it so understands these two aspects of his nature that they may be seen to be complementary, instead of contradictory. By completely reversing the classical procedure and thinking of God as, first of all, the eminently relative One, the new view construes God's absoluteness as simply the abstract structure or identifying principle of his eminent relativity. It is thereby able to show what could never be shown by classical theism, how the Thou with the greatest conceivable degree of real relatedness to others—namely relatedness to *all* others—is for that very reason the most truly absolute Thou any mind can conceive. It can similarly show how maximum temporality entails strict eternity; maximum capacity for change, unsurpassable immutability; and maximum passivity to the action of others, the greatest possible activity in all their numberless processes of self-creation. Ogden, *The Reality of God,* 65.

Attributes of God

	Calvinism	Arminianism	Open Theism	Process Theism
Aseity	God is self-existent, that is, He has the ground of His existence in Himself. . . . The idea of God's self-existence was generally expressed by the term *aseitas,* meaning *self-originated.* . . . As the self-existent God, He is not only independent in Himself, but also causes everything to depend on Him. Berkhof, *Systematic Theology,* 58. If God is self-sufficient does he need to create? In one sense, obviously not. . . . But an individual may be self-sufficient in the sense that nothing else is necessary for that individual's existence and yet he may wish to act or communicate himself, though not because he has a psychological need or deficiency, or some other defect of existence or character such that he has to communicate or create. To want to do something may be a sign not of weakness but of strength, not of deficiency but of fullness. Helm, *Eternal God,* 193.	Whatsoever is predicated absolutely about God, is predicated concerning Him immediately, primarily, and without [respect to] cause. Arminius, *Public Disputations,* IV.XII. *Eternity of Original Cause.*—Science may find an unbroken succession of physical phenomena, in which each is in turn effect and cause, but it cannot find the initiation of the series in physical causation. In the absence of a personal cause, the only alternatives are an infinite series and an uncaused beginning. Neither is thinkable or possible. Reason requires a sufficient cause for a beginning and for the marvelous aggregate of results. God in personality is the only sufficient cause. He must therefore be an eternal personal existence. Miley, *Systematic Theology,* 1:215.	The basic notion which has controlled the development of traditional doctrines of God is the notion of self-sufficiency. The primary, all-explaining being must be self-sufficient, since it must be wholly self-explanatory. The difficulty which arises at once is that though the self-sufficient being is postulated precisely in order to account for the existence of the finite, changing and complex entities of the universe, once one has a self-sufficient being, the existence of anything other than it seems to be unnecessary and superfluous. . . . The way out of this impasse is to reject the doctrine of Divine self-sufficiency. Ward, *Rational Theology and the Creativity of God,* 81. God must not be situated in our thinking . . . so near that he becomes dependent on the world, not by volition but necessarily. Pinnock, *The Openness of God,* 106. Creation is [God's] living space and history the realm of his activity. This does not make God dependent on the world necessarily. Rather it means that God, through grace, has decided to be independent of the world in some respects and dependent on it in other respects. Pinnock, *Most Moved Mover,* 33.	. . . The main point of all such philosophies is that they presuppose individual substance, either one or many individual substances, "which requires nothing but itself in order to exist." This presupposition is exactly what is denied in the more Platonic description which has been given in this lecture. There is no entity, not even God, "which requires nothing but itself in order to exist." . . . Every entity is in its essence social and requires the society in order to exist. Whitehead, *Religion in the Making,* 94. Thus exact analysis shows that we are not obliterating the uniqueness of deity by affirming his relativity. We can even call ours a "negative theology," in that second-order relativity, "relativity of relativity," is in this theology denied of deity, though affirmed of all other beings. God is not, it is true, *simplicicter* "independent"; but the generic manner or universal extent of his dependence is his unique and wholly independent possession. With us, the extent of our dependence is also radically dependent, and our very existence as dependent is wholly a matter of chance or contingency. Hartshorne, *The Divine Relativity,* 82.

Open Theism Compared with Other Theological Systems

Attributes of God

	Calvinism	Arminianism	Open Theism	Process Theism
Immutability	The Immutability of God is the unchangeableness of his essence, attributes, purposes, and consciousness. Immutability results from eternity. . . . That which has no evolution and no succession, is the same yesterday, today, and forever. . . . Immutability belongs to the Divine essence; God can have no new attributes. It belongs also to the Divine will; his decrees are unalterable. Shedd, *Dogmatic Theology,* I:351. God is unchangeable in his essence, attributes, consciousness, and will. All change must be to the better or the worse, but God cannot change to the better, since he is absolutely perfect; neither can he change to the worse, for the same reason. He is exalted above all causes and above even the possibility of change. He can never be wiser, more holy, more just, more merciful, more truthful, nor less so. Nor do his plans and purposes change. The immutability of God is due to the simplicity of his essence. . . . God's immutability is due also to his necessary being and self-existence. Thiessen, *Lectures in Systematic Theology,* 83.	Immutability is a pre-eminent mode of the Essence of God, by which it is void of all change; of being transferred from place to place, because it is itself its own end and good, and because it is immense; of generation and corruption; of alteration; of increase and decrease; for the same reason as that by which it is incapable of suffering. . . . Whence likewise, in the Scriptures, Incorruptibility is attributed to God. Nay, even motion cannot happen to Him through operation; for it appertains to God, and to Him alone, to be at rest in operation. Arminius, *Public Disputations,* IV.XVIII. [God's immutability] excludes all process of becoming, or development, and whatever is meant by change, or the possibility of change. In His essence and in all the attributes of His essential being, God is for ever the same. And of Him alone can this be predicated. . . . Pope, *A Compendium of Christian Theology,* 1:303.	. . . God is not a cosmic stuffed shirt, who is always thinking of himself. Rather he is open to the world and responsive to developments in history. He remembers the past, savors the present and anticipates the future. He is open to new experiences, has a capacity for novelty and is open to reality, which itself is open to change. . . . God is unchangeable with respect to his character, but always changing in relation to us. Pinnock, *Most Moved Mover,* 41. Scripture tells us that God formulates plans and purposes and that he occasionally changes his mind. . . . God repents. Rice, "Biblical Support for a New Perspective"; in Pinnock, *The Openness of God,* 26. It is highly significant that several passages of this "defining" sort list divine repentance (or "relenting," as some translations read) among God's essential characteristics. . . . God does not repent in spite of the fact that he is God; he repents precisely *because* he is God. Rice, "Biblical Support for a New Perspective"; in Pinnock, *The Openness of God,* 31.	Instead of being merely the barren Absolute, which by definition can be really related to nothing, God is in truth related to everything, and that through an immediate sympathetic participation of which our own relation to our bodies is but an image. Similarly, God is no longer thought as utterly unchangeable and empty of all temporal distinctions. Rather, he, too, is understood to be continually in process of self-creation, synthesizing in each new moment of his experience the whole of achieved actuality with the plenitude of possibility as yet unrealized. This implies, naturally, that God is by analogy a living and even growing God and that he is related to the universe of other beings somewhat as the human self is related to its body. Ogden, *The Reality of God,* 59.

Attributes of God

	Calvinism	Arminianism	Open Theism	Process Theism
Immutability	Here an outcry is made by certain men, who, while they dare not openly deny his divinity, secretly rob him of his eternity. For they contend that the Word only began to be when God opened his sacred mouth in the creation of the world. Thus, with excessive temerity, they imagine some change in the essence of God. For as the names of God, which have respect to external work, began to be ascribed to him from the existence of the work, (as when he is called the Creator of heaven and earth,) so piety does not recognize or admit any name which might indicate that a change had taken place in God himself. For if any thing adventitious took place, the saying of James would cease to be true, that "every good gift, and every perfect gift, is from above, and cometh down from the Father of lights, with whom is no variableness, neither shadow of turning," (James 1:17). Nothing, therefore, is more intolerable than to fancy a beginning to that Word which was always God, and afterwards was the Creator of the world. Calvin, *Institutes,* 1.13.8.	[Immutability] is the truth of [God's] eternal absolute identity of being. He is immutable in the plenitude and perfection of his personal attributes. His omniscience, holiness, justice, love, considered simply as attributes, are forever the same . . . In the perfection of his personal attributes God is forever the same. . . . Change within the sphere of expediency is entirely consistent with the unchangeableness of God, while the changeless moral principles are a profound reality of his immutability. . . . The immutability of God . . . arises from the perfection of his personal attributes, and is equally a reality of each, [and] it is not itself an attribute in any distinctive sense. Miley, *Systematic Theology,* 1:221–22.	. . . God's steadfastness will not be seen as a deadening immutability but constancy of character that includes change . . . Pinnock, *Most Moved Mover,* 27. In God's case, we might say that *who God is* does not change but *what God experiences* changes. God's nature does not change but his activities and relationships are dynamic. Pinnock, *Most Moved Mover,* 85. I would say that God is *unchangeable in changeable ways,* i.e. unchangeable in essence but ever changing in the relationships of love that he values. Pinnock, *Most Moved Mover,* 85–86. When Nineveh repented, God's loving character required him to change direction. God's relational consciousness changed when Nineveh repented but his inner being of love remained the same. Pinnock, *Most Moved Mover,* 87.	This absolute character consists in a unique supereminent type of social relations. The divine compassion is not merely, as Anselm said, something in God, other than compassion, which produces upon us the effects of compassion, but is rather an actual sympathy in God. However, in justice to Anselm, we should point out that the unique excellence of the divine sympathetic states does not itself sympathize, is not itself saddened, is never created and cannot be ended or changed by relation to our weal and woe. And this fixed generic excellence is the one eternal causal factor in all good effects, the contrast to all mutability and uncertainty, the one thing which is without possibility of being, or having ever been, otherwise, and which is free of potency, simply and infallibly real. Hartshorne, *The Divine Relativity,* 157.

Open Theism Compared with Other Theological Systems

Attributes of God

	Calvinism	Arminianism	Open Theism	Process Theism
Impassibility	Though [God] is incapable of every feeling of perturbation, he declares that he is angry with the wicked. Wherefore, as when we hear that God is angry, we ought not to imagine that there is any emotion in him, but ought rather to consider the mode of speech accommodated to our sense, God appearing to us like one inflamed and irritated whenever he exercises judgment, so we ought not to imagine any thing more under the term repentance than a change of action, men being wont to testify their dissatisfaction by such a change. Hence, because every change whatever among men is intended as a correction of what displeases, and the correction proceeds from repentance, the same term applied to God simply means that his procedure is changed. In the meantime, there is no inversion of his counsel or will, no change of his affection. What from eternity he had foreseen, approved, decreed, he prosecutes with unvarying uniformity, how sudden soever to the eye of man the variation may seem to be. Calvin, *Institutes,* 1.17.13.	Impassibility is a pre-eminent mode of the Essence of God, according to which it is devoid of all suffering or feeling; not only because nothing can act against this Essence, for it is of infinite Being and devoid of an external cause; but likewise because it cannot receive the act of anything, for it is of simple Entity. Arminius, *Public Disputations,* IV.XVII.	In Scripture, God is revealed as . . . involved in the world most intimately. God does not simply rule over creation, he is moved and affected by what happens in history. Events arouse joy or sorrow, pleasure or wrath in him. Our deeds move, grieve, gladden, or please him. His nature is not characterized merely by intelligence but is also characterized by pathos. Pinnock, *Most Moved Mover,* 55. God seeks a covenantal relationship with his people and can be wounded when it is broken. God is anything but coolly unaffected by what the partners do. Pinnock, *Most Moved Mover,* 56. God hears the cries of his people and mourns over their suffering (Exod. 3:7–8). He even laments over them (Amos 5:1–2). He weeps and wails and mourns. God is deeply involved and not at all removed and detached. Pinnock, *Most Moved Mover,* 57.	. . . Love in the fullest sense involves a sympathetic response to the loved one. Sympathy means feeling the feelings of the other, hurting with the pains of the other, grieving with the grief, rejoicing with the joys. . . . We would doubt that a husband truly loved his wife if his mood did not to some extent reflect hers. Nevertheless, traditional theism said that God is completely impassive, that there was no element of sympathy in the divine love for the creatures. The fact that there was an awareness that this Greek notion of divine impassibility was in serious tension with Biblical notion of divine love for the world is most clearly reflected in this prayer of the eleventh-century theologian Anselm. . . . Cobb, *Process Theology,* 44.

Open Theism Compared with Other Theological Systems

Attributes of God

	Calvinism	Arminianism	Open Theism	Process Theism
Impassibility	1. In his atemporal and nonspatial transcendent existence, God ordains grievous events and evaluates them appropriately. He grieves in that sense, but does not suffer injury or loss. 2. In his temporal and spatial omnipresence, he grieves with his creatures, and he undergoes temporary defeats on his way to the complete victory he has foreordained. 3. In his theophanic presence, he is distressed when his people are distressed (Isa. 63:9), but he promises complete victory and vindication both for himself and for his faithful ones. 4. In the Incarnation, the Son suffers injury and loss: physical pain, deprivation, and death. The Father knows this agony, including the agony of his own separation from his Son. . . . What precise feelings does he experience? We do not know, and we would be wise not to speculate. Frame, *The Doctrine of God,* 614.	The theme of divine reliability is caricatured when stated without reference to other divine qualities, such as mercy, love, and justice. If pressed in isolation from God's character as responsive, empathic, and compassionate, then the assertion of the divine reliability turns easily into an abstract, speculative assertion of divine rigidity and unresponsiveness. . . . The divine constancy does not imply immobility or lack of empathy. Oden, *The Living God,* 111.	Father, Son and Spirit both suffer, though in different ways. The Father suffers the death of his Son and the Spirit feels both the Father's pain and the Son's self-surrender. A God who cannot suffer, as tradition has had it, is less than man and far from the God of the gospel. Pinnock, *Most Moved Mover,* 58. Divine perfection is perfection in change. This is a God who changes and suffers while remaining perfect. Pinnock, *Most Moved Mover,* 58. . . . God is not impassive and unmoved by his creation; rather, in deciding to create us and love us God has opened himself to the possibility of joy and sorrow. . . . Hasker, "A Philosophical Perspective"; in Pinnock, *The Openness of God,* 133–34. If God does only what his nature dictates, then God, being impassible, could never suffer even if he wanted to. But if God cannot even will to suffer, then he is subject to great suffering, since his will is confined. Sanders, "Historical Considerations"; in Pinnock, *The Openness of God,* 76.	Is not the correct ideal rather this, that the parent should be influenced in appropriate, and only in appropriate, ways by the child's desires and fortunes? One should not simply agree to every whim of the child, or strive always to save her from pain or furnish her with pleasure. Nor should one be sunk in misery with her every sorrow, or fantastically elated with her every triumph. But neither should one try to act and think and feel just as one would have acted or thought or felt had the child's joy been sorrow, or her sorrow joy, or her likes dislikes. Yet God, we are told, is impassive and immutable and without accidents, is just as he would be in his action and knowledge and being had we never existed, or had all our experiences been otherwise. Hartshorne, *The Divine Relativity,* 43.

Open Theism Compared with Other Theological Systems

Attributes of God

	Calvinism	Arminianism	Open Theism	Process Theism
Immanence	There is a difference between [God's] physical and his ethical immanence. . . . God's immanence is not an unconscious emanence, but a conscious presence of his being in all his creatures. That is the reason why the nature of this divine presence varies in accordance with the nature of these creatures. To be sure, even the most insignificant creature owes its origin and preservation to God's power, to his being: God dwells in every creature; but this does not mean that he dwells equally in every creature. All things are indeed "*in* him" but all things are not "*with* him." God does not dwell on earth as he dwells in heaven, in animals as in man, in the inorganic as in the organic creation, in the wicked as in the pious, in the church as in Christ. Creatures differ according to the different manner in which God dwells in them. Frame, *The Doctrine of God,* 162–63.	With the immanence of God as the only force operative in nature, we are formally close upon pantheism. . . . The providential agency of God, in whatever sphere of its operation, is purely through his personal will. This cannot be expressed as an organizing and animating divine life in nature. Nor can it be expressed as a force streaming forth at every point in space. . . . God is not operative in his providence as a nature, but only as a person. . . . It follows that the providential agency of God is as purely personal and supernatural in his immanence as in his transcendence. Miley, *Systematic Theology,* 332.	God states in Jeremiah 23:24 that he has taken up residence in the world. . . . Let's not tilt overly to transcendence lest we miss the truth that God is with us in space. Pinnock, *Most Moved Mover,* 32. Perhaps God uses the created order as a kind of body and exercises top-down causation upon it. Pinnock, *Most Moved Mover,* 35.	As the eminent Self, by radical contrast, God's sphere of interaction or body is the whole universe of nondivine beings, with each one of which his relation [is] unsurpassably immediate and direct. His only environment is wholly internal, which means that he can never be localized in any particular space and time, but is omnipresent. Hence, just because God is the *eminently* relative One, there is also a sense in which he is strictly absolute. His being is related to all others [and] is itself relative to nothing, but is the absolute ground of any and all real relationships. Ogden, *The Reality of God,* 60.

Attributes of God

	Calvinism	Arminianism	Open Theism	Process Theism
Immanence	Calvin beyond all question did cherish a very robust faith in the immanence of God. "Our very existence," he says, "is subsistence in God alone." . . . Warfield, *Calvin and Calvinism,* 158. Immanence . . . is basically equivalent to what I called in the last chapter "covenant presence." Frame, *The Doctrine of God,* 105. . . . Divine immanence . . . means that God is present to and in the natural order, human nature, and history. Depending on the conception of God, it may also mean that he is spatiotemporally close to his creation. Feinberg, *No One Like Him,* 59.	This doctrine we call the divine immanence; by which we mean that God is the omnipresent ground of all finite existence and activity. The world . . . is nothing existing and acting on its own account, while God is away in some extra-sidereal region, but it continually depends upon and is ever upheld by the ever-living, ever-present, ever-working God. God's work in nature and history . . . is not against law, but through law. . . . It is not against the laws of mind, but through them, that God realizes his purposes in us. This is an absolute condition of our mental and moral sanity. Thus we see the deep significance of the divine immanence for religious thought. It dispels that great cloud of difficulties . . . that haunt popular religion. . . . It recalls God from the infinite distance in space and time to which sense thought must banish him, and makes him the omnipresent power by which all things exist and on which all things continually depend. This metaphysical presence does not indeed secure spiritual sympathy and fellowship on our part, but it removes the speculative obstacles thereto that exist in many minds, and thus makes room for the spiritual life of communion and sonship. Bowne, "The Immanence of God"; in Langford, ed., *Wesleyan Theology: A Sourcebook,* 152, 155, 160.	By divine immanence I mean that God is everywhere present in all that exists. The world and God are not radically separated realities—God is present within every created being. Pinnock, *The Openness of God,* 111. In relating to us, God communicates and acts in the created order. Sanders, *The God Who Risks,* 24.	He is the binding element in the world. The consciousness which is individual in us, is universal in him: the love which is partial in us is all-embracing in him. Apart from him there could be no world, because there could be no adjustment of individuality. His purpose in the world is quality of attainment. His purpose is always embodied in the particular ideals relevant to the actual state of the world. Thus all attainment is immortal in that it fashions the actual ideals which are God in the world as it is now. Every act leaves the world with a deeper or a fainter impress of God. He then passes into his next relation to the world with enlarged, or diminished, presentation of ideal values. Whitehead, *Religion in the Making,* 143.

Attributes of God

	Calvinism	Arminianism	Open Theism	Process Theism
Transcendence	*Transcendence* invokes the biblical language of God's majesty and holiness. It often represents metaphors of height as well. . . . It refers to God as "the Most High," the one who dwells "above." But since God is not a physical being . . . it is metaphorical to speak of him as living in any place. . . . It is not biblical, therefore, to interpret God's transcendence to mean merely that he is located somewhere far away, in heaven. Frame, *The Doctrine of God,* 104–5. . . . Divine transcendence means that God is separate from and independent of the natural order and human beings. It typically also means that he is superior to anything in our world. . . . Though divine transcendence might suggest a remote God interpersonally, this is not always so. The transcendent God may in fact be very much involved in his creatures' lives. Feinberg, *No One Like Him,* 60.	The attribute of divine immensity suggests that God transcends all spatial relations, while remaining their cause and ground. . . . Oden, *The Living God,* 59. The unlimited presence, knowledge, and influence of God has often been summarized in a single idea: transcendence. Yet transcendence has sometimes been inordinately asserted of God so as to neglect the divine immanence. . . . God is the utterly transcendent One . . . who is nonetheless incomparably present in our midst. . . . Transcendence and immanence are not separable in the Hebraic faith. Oden, *The Living God,* 81.	I maintain that God and the world are ontologically distinct, that God interacts with the world, and that God is omnipotent, omniscient and wholly good. Pinnock, *Most Moved Mover,* 73. The open view sees God as a self-sufficient, ontologically other trinitarian being who voluntarily created the world out of nothing and graciously relates to it in self-limiting ways out of respect for the freedom that he bestowed on the creatures he made. We hold that God is ontologically other than the world and, in a certain sense, "requires" no world. God does not have to relate to some other reality because he is internally social, loving and self-sufficient. Pinnock, *Most Moved Mover,* 145. . . . The open view of God affirms divine transcendence . . . by maintaining that his sensitivity and love are infinitely greater than our own. Rice, "Biblical Support for a New Perspective"; in Pinnock, *The Openness of God,* 42.	The world lives by its incarnation of God in itself. He transcends the temporal world, because He is an actual fact in the nature of things. He is not there as derivative from the world; he is the actual fact from which the other formative elements cannot be torn apart. But equally it stands in his nature that He is the realization of the ideal conceptual harmony by reason of which there is an actual process in the total universe—an evolving world which is actual because there is order. Whitehead, *Religion in the Making,* 140–41. Instead of seeing the reality revealed in Jesus in terms of a predetermined concept of transcendent and omnipotent deity, we must reinterpret deity in the light of what is given us in Jesus. That means that the Creator—Lord of history is not the all-determinative cause of the course of natural and historical events, but a lover of the world who calls it ever beyond what it has attained by affirming life, novelty, consciousness, and freedom again and again. Cobb, *God and the World*, 65.

Attributes of God

	Calvinism	Arminianism	Open Theism	Process Theism
Omniscience	The Divine essence considered as cognizing gives the attribute of Omniscience. . . . The Divine knowledge is (a) Intuitive, as opposed to demonstrative or discursive; it is not obtained by comparing one thing with another, or deducing one truth from another; it is a direct vision. (b) Simultaneous, as opposed to successive; it is not received gradually into the mind, and by parts; the perception is total, and instantaneous. (c) Complete and certain, as opposed to incomplete and uncertain. The Divine knowledge excludes knowledge by the senses, gradual acquisition of knowledge, forgetting of knowledge, and recollection of knowledge. God's omniscience, from the creature's point of view, is foreknowledge; but it is not foreknowledge from God's point of view. The Infinite mind comprehends all things in one simultaneous intuition, and consequently, there is for it no "before," or "after." Shedd, *Dogmatic Theology,* I:354.	The understanding of God is a faculty of his life, which is the first in nature as well as in order, and by which He distinctly understands all things and every thing which now have, will have, have had, can have, or might hypothetically have, any kind of being; by which He likewise distinctly understands the order which all and each of them hold among themselves, the connections and the various relations which they have or can have; not excluding even that entity which belongs to reason, and which exists, or can exist, only in the mind, imagination, and enunciation. Arminius, *Public Disputations,* IV.XXX By omniscience is meant the perfect knowledge which God has of Himself and of all things. It is the infinite perfection of that which in us we call knowledge. Consequently we read that *His understanding is infinite* (Psalm 147:5). God understands and knows the hearts of men. Nothing is hidden from Him. He sees things as they are, in both their causes and ends. Wiley, *Christian Theology,* 1.II.XIV.	. . . God's omniscience will not be seen as know-it-all but as a wisdom which shapes the future in dialogue with creatures. Pinnock, *Most Moved Mover,* 27. Though God knows all there is to know about the world, there are aspects about the future that even God does not know. Though unchangeable with respect to his character and the steadfastness of his purposes, God changes in the light of what happens by interacting with the world. Pinnock, *Most Moved Mover,* 32. . . . If we accept the classical view of foreknowledge and suppose that the Lord was certain that he would *not* let Hezekiah die, wasn't he being duplicitous when he initially told Hezekiah that he would not recover? And if we suppose that the Lord was certain all along that Hezekiah would, in fact, live fifteen years after this episode, wasn't it misleading for God to tell him that he was adding fifteen years to his life? Boyd, *God of the Possible,* 82.	Thus, for example, while creatures have some knowledge, God knows all that can be known. The extreme quantitative difference between human knowledge and divine knowledge makes a qualitative difference, making it possible to conceive of divine omniscience as "all that can be known" without resorting to some absolute difference. But, given the new metaphysics of becoming and creativity, our understanding of "all that can be known" must also be revised. Consistent with the freedom of the creatures and the idea of the universe as genuinely creative process, the future must be regarded as a class without members or as completely nonactual. Thus, future events are in principle unknowable and therefore excluded from the idea of divine omniscience. Reeves, *Process Philosophy and Christian Thought*, 28.

Open Theism Compared with Other Theological Systems

Attributes of God

	Calvinism	Arminianism	Open Theism	Process Theism
Omniscience	Since Scripture includes in the objects of the divine knowledge also the issue of the exercise of freewill on the part of man, the problem arises, how the contingent character of such decisions and the certainty of the divine knowledge can coexist. It is true that the knowledge of God and the purposing will of God are distinct, and that not the former but the latter determines the certainty of the outcome. Consequently the divine omniscience in such cases adds or detracts nothing in regard to the certainty of the event. God's omniscience does not produce but presupposes the certainty by which the problem is raised. At the same time, precisely because omniscience presupposes certainty, it appears to exclude every conception of contingency in the free acts of man, such as would render the latter in their very essence undetermined. The knowledge of the issue must have a fixed point of certainty to terminate upon, if it is to be knowledge at all. Vos, *The International Standard Bible Encyclopedia* Volume 4, 1915 ed., 2191.	The omniscience of God comprehends all things—things past, things present, and things future, and the possible as well as the actual. As set forth in the Bible, the works of God are, as to their time relations, declared to be of the past, of the present, and of the future. By divine arrangement, events do follow in sequence or chronological order. Yet, to God, the things of the past are as real as though now present and the things of the future are as real as though past. . . . Omniscience brings everything—past, present, and future—with equal reality before the mind of God. Strictly speaking, the distinction of foreknowledge in God is a human conception; for divine knowledge is simultaneous as opposed to succession. It is complete and certain as compared to incomplete and uncertain. It is intuitive and not discursive; yet in this perfection of simultaneous, complete, and intuitive knowledge all future events, both possible and real, are cognized by Him. Chafer, *Systematic Theology,* 1:192–93.	. . . God tested Abraham to see what he would do and after the test says through the angel: "Now I know that you fear God" (Gen 22:12). This was a piece of information that God was eager to secure. In another place Moses said that God was testing the people in order to know whether they actually love him or not (Deut 13:3). Pinnock, *The Openness of God,* 122. . . . God expresses frustration: "nor did it enter my mind that they should do this abomination" (Jer 32:35 NSRV). God had not anticipated it. In the book of Jonah . . . [the Ninevites'] repenting was not something God knew in advance would happen. He was planning to destroy them but changed his mind when they converted. Pinnock, *The Openness of God,* 122. . . . God learns things and (I would add) enjoys learning them. . . . God takes delight in the spontaneity of the universe and enjoys continuing to get to know it. . . . Pinnock, *The Openness of God,* 123–24.	. . . An immutably omniscient God . . . would be unjustified in condemning anyone to punishment for sinning. For, from the moment of conception, a person's life could not have been one iota different from its actual course. So the person exercises no freedom in any sense that would justify blame. This conclusion follows merely from the definition of God as an omniscient being who is also immutable in all respects. Griffin, *God, Power and Evil,* 61.

Attributes of God

	Calvinism	Arminianism	Open Theism	Process Theism
Omnipresence	. . . The Divine Omnipresence means rather the presence of all things to God, than God's presence to all things. They are in his presence, but he is not in their presence. . . . The omnipresence of God is not like the presence of a material body in a locality. . . . The Divine omnipresence is not like the presence of a finite spirit embodied in a material form. . . . The omnipresence of God is not by extension, multiplication, or division of essence. . . . The whole essence of God is here, is there, and everywhere. Shedd, *Dogmatic Theology,* I:340-41.	After creatures, and places in which creatures are contained, have been granted to have an existence, from this Immensity follows the Omnipresence or Ubiquity of the Essence of God, according to which it is entirely wheresoever any creature or any place is, and this in exact similarity to a [mathematical] point, which is totally present to the entire circumference, and to each of its parts, and yet without circumscription. If there be any difference, it arises, from the Will, the Ability and the Act of God. Arminius, *Public Disputations,* IV.XVI.	I do not feel obliged to assume that God is a purely spiritual being when his self-revelation does not suggest it. It is true that from a Platonic standpoint, the idea is absurd, but this is not a biblical standpoint. And how unreasonable is it anyway? The only persons we encounter are embodied persons and, if God is not embodied, it may prove difficult to understand how God is a person. What kind of actions could a disembodied God perform? Embodiment may be the way in which the transcendent God is able to be immanent and why God is presented in such terms. I would say that God transcends the world, while being able to indwell it. Pinnock, *Most Moved Mover,* 34–35.	. . . God is not simply *an* exemplification of metaphysical principles, but is their *"chief"* exemplification. So, whereas the human self is effectively related only to a very few others—indeed, only to a very few others within the intimate world of its own body—the divine Self is effectively related to *all* others in such a way that there are no gradations of intimacy of the various creatures to it. God is not located in a particular space and time, but rather is omnipresent and eternal, in the sense that he is directly present to all spaces and times and they to him. Ogden, *The Reality of God,* 175–76.

Attributes of God

	Calvinism	Arminianism	Open Theism	Process Theism
Omnipresence	. . . If [God] is omnipresent in space and time, he cannot be a particular physical being, for no such being could inhabit all times and places equally. . . . God is present in the world he has made. In his immanent temporal and spatial omnipresence, God experiences the world in ways similar to the ways we do. . . . God experiences the world . . . from every particular perspective within the universe. Frame, *The Doctrine of God,* 584–85.	Immensity is a pre-eminent mode of the Essence of God, by which it is void of place according to space and limits: being co-extended space, because it belongs to simple entity, not having part and part, therefore not having part beyond part. Being also its own encircling limits, or beyond which it has no existence, because it is of infinite entity: and, before all things, God alone was both the world, and place, and all things to himself; but He was alone, because there was nothing outwardly beyond, except himself. Arminius, *Public Disputations,* IV.XV.	In tradition, God is thought to function primarily as a disembodied spirit but this is scarcely a biblical idea. For example, Israel is called to hear God's word and gaze on his glory and beauty. Human beings are said to be embodied creatures created in the image of God. Is there perhaps something in God that corresponds with embodiment? Having a body is certainly not a negative thing because it makes it possible for us to be agents. Perhaps God's agency would be easier to envisage if he were in some way corporeal. Pinnock, *Most Moved Mover,* 33–34. The only personal agents we know about are embodied agents. It might help us to imagine divine agency if God were somehow, mysteriously, embodied. It might also explain the divine passibility and even divine omniscience if God could access feelings of ours and his own. It would also overcome the spirit-matter dualism that so impoverished our sense of God's sacramental presence in the church. . . . The world is surely not God's body in the way we experience it. Pinnock, *Most Moved Mover,* 81.	There is no religious objection to this understanding of God as nonspatial, and it is probable that Whitehead himself held it, but I find it more intelligible to say that God is everywhere. In the first instance this means, what adherents of the other view also hold, that God is immediately related to every place, that there is nowhere one can flee from him. Certainly it agrees with the first view in the insistence that God is no more at one place than another and that, when space is conceived visually, it fails to apply to God. But the visual understanding of space has been overcome also in physics without the abandonment of the idea of space in general. Cobb, *God and the World,* 77.

Attributes of God

	Calvinism	Arminianism	Open Theism	Process Theism
Omnipotence	And truly God claims omnipotence to himself, and would have us to acknowledge it, — not the vain, indolent, slumbering omnipotence which sophists feign, but vigilant, efficacious, energetic, and ever active, — not an omnipotence which may only act as a general principle of confused motion, as in ordering a stream to keep within the channel once prescribed to it, but one which is intent on individual and special movements. God is deemed omnipotent, not because he can act though he may cease or be idle, or because by a general instinct he continues the order of nature previously appointed; but because, governing heaven and earth by his providence, he so overrules all things that nothing happens without his counsel. For when it is said in the Psalms, "He has done whatsoever he has pleased," (Psalm 115:3), the thing meant is his sure and deliberate purpose. It were insipid to interpret the Psalmist's words in philosophic fashion, to mean that God is the primary agent, because the beginning and cause of all motion. Calvin, *Institutes,* 1.16.3.	The Power of God is infinite; because it can do not only all things possible; (which are innumerable, so that they cannot be reckoned to be such a number, without a possibility of their being still more;) but likewise because nothing can resist it. For all created things depend upon the Divine Power, as upon their efficient principle, as the phrase is, both in their being and in their preservation; whence Omnipotence is deservedly attributed to Him. Arminius, *Public Disputations,* IV.LXXXIII The omnipotence of God is the ground of all that we call efficiency or causality. It is related to the absolute attribute of Aseity as personality expressed in will, and to the omnipresence of God, as Aseity related to the creature. Being an expression of the divine will, it is also directly and vitally connected with the moral attributes of God. Omnipotence is rightly defined as that perfection of God by virtue of which He is able to do all that He pleases to do. Wiley, *Christian Theology,* 1.II.XIV.	It may still be objected that a granting of real freedom to creatures may involve a thwarting of God's purposes, since creatures may not do what God wants them to do. They will accordingly limit his power, and it will no longer be true that "God's will inevitably is always fulfilled." . . . That is so. . . . Ward, *Rational Theology and the Creativity of God,* 83. *Why* cannot God, the omnipotent Creator, do whatever he wants, wherever he wants, however he wants? . . . The answer would be that love involves freedom . . . and that freedom involves genuinely open alternatives and thus genuine risks. . . . In every situation, then, God must contend with the quality of irrevocable freedom he has given to each agent, together with all the contingent variables that condition each agent's quality of freedom. Boyd, *Satan and the Problem of Evil,* 212–13.	If we think, then, of God's power as persuasive power, we may still use the term "omnipotence" if we like, but its meaning is quite altered. It no longer means that God exercises a monopoly of power and compels everything to be just as it is. It means instead that he exercies the optimum persuasive power in relation to whatever is. Such an optimum is a balance between urging toward the good and maximizing the power—therefore the freedom—of the one whom God seeks to persuade. Cobb, *God and the World,* 90.

Attributes of God

	Calvinism	Arminianism	Open Theism	Process Theism
Omnipotence	The power of God . . . is nothing other than the divine essence itself productive outwardly (through which he is conceived as able to do whatsoever he wills or can will). . . . This comes to be distinguished from such a power or *exousia* as implies the right and authority to do anything, while the power of which we speak indicates in its conception only the force and faculty of acting. Turretin, *Institutes of Elenctic Theology,* 1.3.21.I. The object of God's power is nothing other than the possible, i.e., whatever is not repugnant to be done. . . . But the impossible falls not under the omnipotence of God, not from a defect in his power, but from a defect in the possibility of the thing because it involves in its conception contradictory predicates. Turretin, *Institutes of Elenctic Theology,* 1.3.21.VI.	Those things are impossible to God which involve a contradiction, as, to make another God, to be mutable, to sin, to lie, to cause some thing at once to be and not to be, to have been and not to have been, &c., that this thing should be and not be, that it and its contrary should be, that an accident should be without its subject, that a substance should be changed into a pre-existing substance, bread into the body of Christ, that a body should possess ubiquity, &c. These things partly belong to a want of power to be capable of doing them, and partly to a want of will to do them. Arminius, *Private Disputations,* XXII.V. But the capability of God is infinite—and this not only because it can do all things possible, which, indeed, are innumerable, so that as many cannot be enumerated as it is capable of doing, [or after all that can be numbered, it is capable of doing still more]; nor can such great things be calculated without its being able to produce far greater, but likewise because nothing can resist it. For all created things depend upon him, as upon the efficient principle, both in their being and in their preservation. Hence, omnipotence is justly ascribed to him. Arminius, *Private Disputations,* XXII.VI.	. . . It might help if we think of God's power and our say-so in terms of percentages. Prior to creation, God possessed 100 percent of all power. He possessed all the say-so there was. When the Trinity decided to express their love by bringing forth a creation, they invested each creature (angelic and human) with a certain percentage of their say-so. The say-so of the triune God was at this point no longer the only one that determined how things would go. God's personal creations now possessed a measure of ability to influence what would occur. Boyd, *God of the Possible,* 97. . . . God cannot just do anything he wants, when he wants to. . . . His power can, at least temporarily, be blocked and his will not be done in the short term. Pinnock, *Most Moved Mover,* 135. In the open view, it is possible to question God's wisdom and the ways in which he is employing his power. Pinnock, *Most Moved Mover,* 137.	Instead of saying that God's power is limited, suggesting that it is less than some conceivable power, we should rather say: his power is absolutely maximal, the greatest possible, but even the greatest possible power is still one power among others, is not the only power. God can do everything that a God can do, everything that could be done by "a being with no possible superior." In another manner of speaking, we may say that deity is the absolute case of social influence; but even the absolute case of such influence is still—social. This means, it takes account of the freedom of others, and determines events only by setting appropriate limits to the self-determining of others, of the local agents. Hartshorne, *The Divine Relativity,* 138.

Open Theism Compared with Other Theological Systems

Attributes of God

	Calvinism	Arminianism	Open Theism	Process Theism
Sovereignty	Hence we maintain, that by his providence, not heaven and earth and inanimate creatures only, but also the counsels and wills of men are so governed as to move exactly in the course which he has destined. Calvin, *Institutes,* 1.16.8. Sovereignty is not a property of the divine nature, but a prerogative arising out of the perfections of the Supreme Being. If God be a Spirit, and therefore a person, infinite, eternal, and immutable in his being and perfections, the Creator and Preserver of the universe, He is of right its absolute sovereign. Hodge, *Systematic Theology,* 1.V.15.	My sentiments respecting the providence of God are these: It is present with, and presides over, all things; and all things, according to their essences, quantities, qualities, relations, actions, passions, places, times, stations and habits, are subject to its governance, conservation, and direction. . . . And, what is still more, I do not take away from the government of the divine providence even sins themselves, whether we take into our consideration their commencement, their progress, or their termination. Arminius, *A Letter to Hippolytus Collibus,* chap. II, Introduction. The power of God serves universally, and at all times, to execute these acts, with the exception of permission; specially, and sometimes, these acts are executed by the creatures themselves. Hence, an act of providence is called either immediate or mediate. When it employs [the agency of] the creatures, then it permits them to conduct their motions agreeably to their own nature, unless it be his pleasure to do any thing out of the ordinary way. Arminius, *Private Disputations,* XXVIII.VIII.	Open theists rather maintain that God can and does predetermine and foreknow *whatever he wants to* about the future. . . . God is so confident in his sovereignty, we hold, he does not need to micromanage everything. He could if he wanted to, but this would demean his sovereignty. So he chooses to leave some of the future open to possibilities, allowing them to be resolved by the decisions of free agents. Boyd, *God of the Possible,* 31. . . . In the open view things can happen to us that have no overarching divine purpose. In this view, "trusting in God" provides no assurance that everything that happens to us will reflect his divine purposes, for there are other agents who also have power to affect us, just as we have power to affect others. Boyd, *God of the Possible,* 153. . . . God is not viewed as being completely in control and exercising exhaustive sovereignty. . . . God controls some things, but not everything. He conducts a "general" rather than a "meticulous" sovereignty. Pinnock, *Most Moved Mover,* 53.	[The Galilean origin of Christianity] does not emphasize the ruling Caesar, or the ruthless moralist, or the unmoved mover. It dwells upon the tender elements in the world, which slowly and in quietness operate by love; and it finds purpose in the present immediacy of a kingdom not of this world. Love neither rules, nor is it unmoved; also it is a little oblivious as to morals. It does not look to the future; for it finds its own reward in the immediate present. Whitehead, *Process and Reality,* 520–21.

Open Theism Compared with Other Theological Systems

Attributes of God

	Calvinism	Arminianism	Open Theism	Process Theism
Sovereignty	There is a twofold consideration of providence, according to its twofold object and manner of dispensation; the one is general, exercised about all creatures, rational and irrational, animate and inanimate; the other *special* and peculiar. Christ hath an universal empire over all things, Eph. i. 22. The head of the whole world by way of *dominion;* but an head to the church by way of *union* and *special influence,* John xvii. 2 . . . The church is his *special* care and charge; he rules the world for her good, as an head consulting the welfare of the body. Flavel, *The Works of John Flavel,* IV:350.	Providential GOVERNMENT is limited to intelligent or probationary creatures. It is a vague use of the term government which applies it to the control of all things: there is no rule, worthy of being connected with the name of the Supreme, save over free beings, conscious of their freedom and of their responsibility. Similarly, the word strictly belongs to the control of God over probationary creatures, that is, over beings undergoing a temporary trial with reference to an eternal issue. Pope, *A Compendium of Christian Theology,* 1:452.	. . . Don't we normally regard someone who refuses to take risks as being insecure? Don't we ordinarily regard a compulsion to meticulously control everything as evidencing weakness, not strength? Of course we do. Everyone who is psychologically healthy knows it is good to risk loving another person, for example. You may, of course, get hurt, for people are free agents. But the risk-free alternatives of not loving or of trying to control another person is evidence of insecurity and weakness, if not sickness. Why should we abandon this insight when we think about God, especially since Scripture clearly depicts God as sometimes taking risks? Boyd, *God of the Possible,* 57–58.	. . . The problem of evil does not disappear when we think of God in this way, but it loses much of its force. The world is not seen any longer as embodying an omnipotent sovereign's will but rather as responding ever anew to the possibility offered. That the response is imperfect does not imply the imperfection of what is offered. There is no world that does not reflect the influence of God's past agency, but there is also no world that is the product of that agency alone. The terrible reality of evil is neither denied nor attributed to God. Cobb, *God and the World,* 64.

Open Theism Compared with Other Theological Systems

Attributes of God

	Calvinism	Arminianism	Open Theism	Process Theism
Relationship to Creation	The carnal mind, when once it has perceived the power of God in the creation, stops there, and, at the farthest, thinks and ponders on nothing else than the wisdom, power, and goodness displayed by the Author of such a work, (matters which rise spontaneously, and force themselves on the notice even of the unwilling,) or on some general agency on which the power of motion depends, exercised in preserving and governing it. In short, it imagines that all things are sufficiently sustained by the energy divinely infused into them at first. But faith must penetrate deeper. After learning that there is a Creator, it must forthwith infer that he is also a Governor and Preserver, and that, not by producing a kind of general motion in the machine of the globe as well as in each of its parts, but by a special providence sustaining, cherishing, superintending, all the things which he has made, to the very minutest, even to a sparrow. Calvin, *Institutes,* 1.16.1.	The providence of God is subordinate to creation; and it is, therefore, necessary that it should not impinge against creation, which it would do, were it to inhibit or hinder the use of free will in man, or should deny to man its necessary concurrence, or should direct man to another end, or to destruction, than to that which is agreeable to the condition and state in which he was created; that is, if the providence of God should so rule and govern man that he should necessarily become corrupt, in order that God might manifest his own glory, both of justice and mercy, through the sin of man, according to his eternal counsel. Arminius, *Certain Articles to be Diligently Examined,* VIII.1.	On the grandest scale, creation as a whole is itself God's partner. . . . But it is also a world in jeopardy with forces at work that resist God and a power of chaos that hinders the blessing of God. The acts of creation as recorded in Genesis chapter 1 brought chaos under control and reintroduced God's order, but they did not eliminate the threat of this mysterious "formless void" factor (v. 2). It is a situation where, although God has the upper hand, he is not now totally in control. Scripture presents God as engaged in conflict with powers of darkness. The tradition has presented an all too serene picture of the situation, where God does not have to struggle with any opposing power. Creation is God's partner not just a passive product. Pinnock, *Most Moved Mover,* 36.	Process theology sees God's fundamental aim to be the promotion of the creatures' own enjoyment. God's creative influence upon them is loving, because it aims at promoting that which the creatures experience as intrinsically good. Since God is not in complete control, the divine love is not contradicted by the great amount of intrinsic evil, or "disenjoyment" in the world. The creatures in part create both themselves and their successors. Cobb, *Process Theology*, 56.

Open Theism Compared with Other Theological Systems

Attributes of God

	Calvinism	Arminianism	Open Theism	Process Theism
Relationship to Creation	If the fact that men can use the laws of nature to their "own ends and advantages" is compatible with the uniformity of those laws, the control of God over them for the accomplishment of his purposes cannot be inconsistent with their stability as laws. God rules the creation in accordance with the laws which He himself has ordained. Hodge, *Systematic Theology,* 1.XI.4.A. . . . Men owe God their obedience simply on the basis of the Creator-creature relationship existing between them. . . . It is *not* on the basis of the covenant of works which God established with Adam . . . that mankind acquired the obligation to serve God. Even if he had done nothing more for them than to sustain them by his ordinary providence and to tell them what they had to do to please him, Adam and his descendants would still have been under obligation to Him as their Creator to render him all due obedience as his rational creatures. Reymond, *A New Systematic Theology of the Christian Faith,* 404.	And it may be defined the solicitous, everywhere powerful, and continued inspection and oversight of God, according to which he exercises a general care over the whole world, and over each of the creatures and their actions and passions, in a manner that is befitting himself, and suitable for his creatures, for their benefit, especially for that of pious men, and for a declaration of the divine perfection. Arminius, *Private Disputations,* XVIII.IV. From an inspection of the matter and form, it is evident, First, that creation is the immediate act of God, alone, both because a creature, who is of a finite power is incapable of operating on nothing, and because such a creature cannot shape matter in substantial forms. Secondly. The creation was freely produced, not necessarily, because God was neither bound to nothing, nor destitute of forms. Arminius, *Private Disputations,* XXIV.VII.	God has bound himself to his creation. . . . God chooses not to exercise judgment without the human input of this man he trusts. . . . It is clear that God considers others as having something significant to say. Sanders, *The God Who Risks,* 53. God's project involves the creation of significant others who are ontologically distinct from himself and upon whom he showers his caring love in the expectation that they will respond in love. . . . Prior to creation, even if God had no warrant to believe anything would go amiss, there existed the "implausible possibility" that resistance to the divine purpose might arise. . . . God freely chooses to be affected by his creatures—there is contingency in God's relation with creation. Sanders, *The God Who Risks,* 169. God's decision to make this kind of world constrains his freedom to act. . . . Creation placed limits on God's freedom to act subsequently. As Creator, God cannot and will not scrap the conditions . . . which underlie the project. Pinnock, *Most Moved Mover,* 136.	God's role is not the combat of productive force with productive force, of destructive force with destructive force; it lies in the patient operation of the overpowering rationality of his conceptual harmonization. He does not create the world, he saves it: or, more accurately, he is the poet of the world, with tender patience leading it by his vision of truth, beauty, and goodness. Whitehead, *Process and Reality,* 525–26.

Related Theological Issues

	Calvinism	Arminianism	Open Theism	Process Theism
Human Free Will	All this being admitted, it will be beyond dispute, that free will does not enable any man to perform good works, unless he is assisted by grace; indeed, the special grace which the elect alone receive through regeneration. Calvin, *Institutes,* 2.2.6. In this way, then, man is said to have free will, not because he has a free choice of good and evil, but because he acts voluntarily, and not by compulsion. This is perfectly true: but why should so small a matter have been dignified with so proud a title? An admirable freedom! that man is not forced to be the servant of sin, while he is, however, ἐθελοδουλος (ethelodoulos, a voluntary slave); his will being bound by the fetters of sin. Calvin, *Institutes,* 2.2.7.	The liberty of the will consists in this — when all the requisites for willing or not willing are laid down, man is still indifferent to will or not to will, to will this rather than that. This indifference is removed by the previous determination, by which the will is circumscribed and absolutely determined to the one part or to the other of the contradiction or contrariety; and this predetermination, therefore, does not consist with the liberty of the will, which requires not only free capability, but also free use in the very exercise of it. Arminius, *Certain Articles to be Diligently Examined,* VI.8.	The open view of God also has appeal because it resonates with and affirms the human intuition that there is freedom. This is important because freedom is part of the God-human relationship, which is personal and mutual, not manipulative or causal. Pinnock, *Most Moved Mover,* 160. . . . God is restricted in terms of what he can unilaterally carry out by the domain of irrevocable freedom he has given to agents. Boyd, *Satan and the Problem of Evil,* 231. It is incumbent on the incompatibilist to make clear what it is that divine foreknowledge is incompatible *with.* The notion of free will involved here is nicely expressed by David Basinger when he says that when a person is free to perform an action, she "has it in her power to choose to perform A or choose not to perform A. *Both A and not A could actually occur;* which *will* actually occur has *not yet been determined.*" ["Middle Knowledge and Classical Christian Thought," *Religious Studies* 22 (1986): 416.] Hasker, *God, Time, and Knowledge,* 66.	What then is this cosmic status? Is it power to get local agents to do anything they could do, power to make or cause them to do it? No, for in spite of what Thomists say, it is impossible that our act should be both free and yet a logical consequence of a divine action which "infallibly" produces its effect. Power to cause someone to perform by his own choice an act precisely defined by the cause is meaningless. The cause can set conditions more or less favorable to such a choice; but if it is a choice, then, in spite of these conditions, the choice is not in all aspects inevitable and may not occur. Hartshorne, *The Divine Relativity,* 135.

Open Theism Compared with Other Theological Systems

Related Theological Issues

	Calvinism	Arminianism	Open Theism	Process Theism
Human Free Will	. . . I shall consider the notion of a self-determining power in the will: wherein, according to the Arminians, does most essentially consist the will's freedom; and shall particularly inquire, whether it be not plainly absurd, and a manifest inconsistence, to suppose that the will itself determines all the free acts of the will. Edwards, *The Works of Jonathan Edwards: The Freedom of the Will,* 171. Upon the whole, I presume there is no person of good understanding, who impartially considers the things which have been observed, but will allow that 'tis not evident from the dictates of the common sense, or natural notions of mankind, that moral necessity is inconsistent with praise and blame. And therefore, if the Arminians would prove any such inconsistency, it must be by some philosophical and metaphysical arguments, and not common sense. Edwards, *The Works of Jonathan Edwards: Freedom of the Will,* 363.	The word, arbitrium, "choice," or "free will," properly signifies both the faculty of the mind or understanding, by which the mind is enabled to judge about any thing proposed to it, and the judgment itself which the mind forms according to that faculty. But it is transferred from the Mind to the Will on account of the very close connection which subsists between them. Liberty, when attributed to the will, is properly an affection of the will, though it has its root in the understanding and reason. Generally considered, it is various. (1.) It is a Freedom from the control or jurisdiction of one who commands, and from an obligation to render obedience. (2.) From the inspection, care, and government of a superior. (3.) It is also a freedom from necessity, whether this proceeds from an external cause compelling, or from a nature inwardly determining absolutely to one thing. (4.) It is a freedom from sin and its dominion. (5.) And a freedom from misery. Arminius, *Public Disputations,* XI.I.	. . . Humans, as personal beings, have the ability to say yes or no to God's love. Love cannot be forced. Consequently, even though God wants us to respond with a yes so that we enter into a relationship of mutual love, such a response cannot be coerced. Sanders, *The God Who Risks,* 209. . . . No being, not even God, can know in advance precisely what free agents will do, even though he may predict it with great accuracy. My assumption is, and the Bible seems to share it, that exhaustive foreknowledge would not be possible in a world with real freedom. Pinnock, *Most Moved Mover,* 100. Whether we love God or not, whether we cooperate with God or not, are genuinely free decisions. God cannot push a button and make a human person love him. Pinnock, *Most Moved Mover,* 158.	Central to existential thought is the formal doctrine that existence precedes essence. What we are as human beings is not decided for us by God, by society, or by our own personal past. We decide in the act of existing. We may try to evade the radical responsibility that this places upon us, but such evasion is itself a decision as to what we are. Furthermore, there are no preestablished rules that either factually or normatively govern our existence. Each situation is unique. If we choose to apply a rule, that is the choice for which we are responsible. There is no predetermined end toward which we are directed. The future is radically open. We create the future in our decision. We are responsible for the future. To all this a Whiteheadian agrees. Cobb, *Process Theology,* 81.

Open Theism Compared with Other Theological Systems

Related Theological Issues

	Calvinism	Arminianism	Open Theism	Process Theism
Human Free Will	(1.) In the ordinary operations or acts of free agents, the ability to perform them belongs to the agent and arises out of his nature as a rational creature. . . . Whereas the acts of faith, repentance, and other holy affections do not flow from the ability of men in the present condition of their nature, but from a new principle of life supernaturally communicated and maintained. (2.) The ordinary acts of men, and especially their wicked acts, are determined by their own natural inclinations and feelings. God does not awaken, or infuse those feelings or dispositions in order to determine sinners to act wickedly. On the other hand, all gracious or holy affections are thus infused or excited by the Spirit of God. (3.) The providential government of God over free agents is exercised as much in accordance with the laws of mind, as his providential government over the material world is in accordance with the established laws of matter. Both belong to the *potentia ordinata,* or ordered efficiency of God. This is not the case in the operations of his grace. Hodge, *Systematic Theology,* 1.XI.4.B.	. . . All the drawings of the Father; the desires after God, which, if we yield to them, increase more and more;—all that light wherewith the Son of God "enlighteneth every one that cometh into the world"; . . . all the convictions which his Spirit, from time to time, works in every child of man; although, it is true, the generality of men stifle them as soon as possible . . . Wesley, *The Works of John Wesley,* Sermon XLIII, 44. Sin, or the separation of the created will from the will of God, was foreseen by the Creator. . . . It was permitted. . . . No Divine restraint was laid upon the freedom of the creature in that possibility of its direction which was towards departure from God. Pope, *A Compendium of Christian Theology,* 453.	The libertarian or incompatibilist view holds that "an agent is free with respect to a given action at a given time if at that time it is within the agent's power to perform the action and also in the agent's power to refrain from the action." Libertarians do not ignore genetics or environmental factors that influence decisions, but they maintain that a person could have done otherwise than she did in any given situation. Sanders, *The God Who Risks,* 221. Much of what we will do tomorrow is already determined because of our genes, environment, commitments, the character we've acquired thus far, and so on. But at least some of what we will do tomorrow is not settled. Boyd, *God of the Possible,* 110. Total knowledge of the future would imply a fixity of events. Nothing in the future would need to be decided. It also would imply that human freedom is an illusion, that we make no difference and are not responsible. Pinnock, *The Openness of God,* 121.	

Related Theological Issues

	Calvinism	Arminianism	Open Theism	Process Theism
Hermeneutics	We must not rashly and unnecessarily depart from the proper literal sense, unless it really clashes with the articles of faith and the precepts of love and the passage (on this account or from other parallel passages) is clearly seen to be figurative. Turretin, *Institutes of Elenctic Theology*, 1.2.19.XIX. The Scripture's own doctrine of Scripture has three implications for biblical hermeneutics: *First, the Scripture's doctrine of Scripture, espousing its own revelatory and inspired character, binds us to the grammatical/historical method of exegesis. . . . Second, the Scripture's doctrine of Scripture commits us to the harmonization of Scripture. . . . Third, and finally, despite the "occasional" or* ad hoc *character of its many literary parts, the Scripture's doctrine of Scripture binds us to view its teachings as timeless truths intended for "our instruction, reproof, correction, and training in righteousness."* Reymond, *A New Systematic Theology of the Christian Faith*, 49–52.	We do not wish to introduce unbounded license, by which it may be allowable to any person, whether a public interpreter of Scripture or a private individual, to reject, without cause, any interpretations whatsoever, whether made by one prophet, or by more; but we desire the liberty of prophesying [or public expounding] to be preserved entire and unimpaired in the church. This liberty, itself, however, we subject to the judgment of God, as possessing the power of life and death, and to that of the church, or of her prelates who are endowed with the power of binding and loosing. Arminius, *Private Disputations*, IX.XIII.	If our thinking about the conditions of love contradict our reading of Scripture, for example, this is a sure indication that we are either reasoning improperly or interpreting the Bible incorrectly. Similarly, if our interpretation of Scripture contradicts our experience, this also is a sure indication that we are either misinterpreting Scripture or our experience. And when aspects of the church's theological tradition come into conflict with either Scripture, reason or experience, this too is an indication that we need to question either the church's tradition or our use of these other three criteria. Boyd, *Satan and the Problem of Evil*, 22. The classical view is so taken for granted that it functions as a preunderstanding that rules out certain interpretations of Scripture, since they do not "fit" with the conception of what is thought "appropriate" for God to be like. Sanders, *The God Who Risks*, 141–42. The emergence of a more dynamic view of reality allows people to read the Bible better and even do philosophy in new ways. Pinnock, *Most Moved Mover*, 121.	David Griffin has proposed and described in numerous writings a "constructive" postmodern project, which does not give in to the relativism and the endless ungrounded signification of deconstructive postmodernism, but rather advocates the systematic engagement of reality through the formation and testing of "propositions" in the Whiteheadian sense. It is the central role of the "proposition" that distinguishes process hermeneutics as such. For Whitehead, a proposition was not, as for evangelicals like Carl Henry and for many secular philosophers of language, a verifiable linguistic transcript of a state of affairs in the world. Rather it was a "lure to creative emergence in the transcendent future." . . . In other words, it is oriented toward the free subject's self-creation in the reality and possibility of its own situation—not so different, really from the "call to faithful discipleship" endemic to classical Christianity, particularly when that call is interpreted eschatologically (cf. "the transcendent future") as has been done increasingly by contemporary Protestant thinkers. . . . Wheeler, in Pinnock, *Searching for an Adequate God*, 129.

Related Theological Issues

	Calvinism	Arminianism	Open Theism	Process Theism
Hermeneutics	If we are to avoid hermeneutical nihilism, we must avoid mistakes to which many twentieth-century exegetes are prone. Besides acknowledging the inescapability of presuppositional interpretation, we must affirm the indispensable importance of valid exegetical assumptions. . . . The Word of God is therefore not objectively inaccessible, but is conveyed in intelligible human speech, and its truth given in universally valid statements; it is not conditioned upon private decision or subjective response. . . . We must champion the indispensable importance of historical and philological exegesis in identifying the content of the scripturally given revelation, and must acknowledge that authorial cognitive intention is ultimately definitive for textual meaning. Henry, *God, Revelation and Authority,* IV.3.314.	But the authority of no one is so great, whether it be that of an individual or of a church, as to be able to obtrude his own interpretation on the people as the authentic one. From this affirmation however, by way of eminence, we except the prophets and the apostles. For such interpretation is always subjected to the judgment of him to whom it is proposed, to this extent — that he is bound to receive it, only so far as it is confirmed by strength of arguments. . . . Arminius, *Private Disputations,* IX.XI, XIII.	Where the open view and the classical view differ in their treatment of passages such as these is that the open view does not read into these verses the *assumption* that the future must be exhaustively settled. Boyd, *God of the Possible,* 42. The open view of God proposes to take biblical metaphors more seriously and thereby recover the dynamic and relational God of the gospel, but in doing so it runs the risk of being too literal in its interpretation. Pinnock, *Most Moved Mover,* 60–61. The problem with the tradition is not that it takes the biblical language metaphorically rather than literally but that it bypasses truths conveyed by it. Pinnock, *Most Moved Mover,* 63.	In other words, one can actually verify mythical assertions only by following the twofold hermeneutical procedure that Bultmann has called "demythologizing." Such assertions can never be verified directly but must always be handled like other assertions involving a "category mistake"; they must be taken not literally but symbolically and so interpreted as, in Ryle's words, to reallocate the "facts" of which they speak to another more appropriate "idiom." This means, specifically, that mythical utterances must be interpreted so as to disclose the answer they give to the question of faith and that this answer must then be restated in terms in which such answers can be literally and properly given. Only after both of these steps have been taken can one actually determine whether a mythical assertion is true. For the truth of such an assertion is like that of a metaphor: it is really the truth of the understanding of faith of which the assertion itself is but an inadequate symbol. Ogden, *The Reality of God,* 118–19.

Related Theological Issues

	Calvinism	Arminianism	Open Theism	Process Theism
Suffering	If there is no more effectual remedy for anger and impatience, he assuredly has not made little progress who has learned so to meditate on Divine Providence, as to be able always to bring his mind to this, The Lord willed it, it must therefore be born; not only because it is unlawful to strive with him, but because he wills nothing that is not just and befitting. The whole comes to this. When unjustly assailed by men, overlooking their malice, (which could only aggravate our grief, and whet our minds for vengeance,) let us remember to ascend to God, and learn to hold it for certain, that whatever an enemy wickedly committed against us was permitted, and sent by his righteous dispensation. Calvin, *Institutes,* 1.17.8.	If it be . . . inquired, why [the righteous] are persecuted, the answer is equally plain and obvious. It is "for righteousness' sake"; because they are righteous. . . . Whatever may be pretended, this is the real cause: be their infirmities more or less, still, if it were not for this, they would be borne with, and the world would love its own. They are persecuted because they are *poor in spirit.* . . . The reason is plain: the spirit which is in the world is directly opposite to the Spirit which is of God. It must therefore needs be that those who are of the world will be opposite to those who are of God. Wesley, "Sermon XVIII: Upon Our Lord's Sermon on the Mount," III.III.3–4; in Sugden, *John Wesley's Fifty-Three Sermons.*	. . . The trinitarian warfare theodicy contrasts with theodicies predicated on the blueprint worldview, that is, that assume there must always be a specific divine reason for each specific evil in the world. I do not deny that in the context of this war zone God *sometimes* may allow, or even ordain, suffering for a particular higher purpose. . . . However, I deny that Scripture, reason or experience requires the belief that suffering must *always* serve a divine purpose. Boyd, *Satan and the Problem of Evil,* 19. . . . The apologetic need for a warfare perspective on suffering and evil will not be seen if there is an insufficient appreciation for the radicality of evil in our world and the radical nature of the problem this poses for the classical-philosophical understanding of divine sovereignty as meticulous control. Many times this radicality is not appreciated in contemporary discussions on the problem of evil, a fact that contributes to a pervasive willingness to accept shallow explanations for why evil occurs. Boyd, *God at War,* 32.	

Related Theological Issues

	Calvinism	Arminianism	Open Theism	Process Theism
Suffering	The sufferings of life, which are the result of the entrance of sin into the world, are also included in the penalty of sin. Sin brought disturbance into the entire life of man. His physical life fell prey to weaknesses and diseases, which result in discomforts and often in agonizing pains; and his mental life became subject to distressing disturbances, which often rob him of the joy of life, disqualify him for his daily task, and sometimes entirely destroy his mental equilibrium. . . . Man is in a state of dissolution, which often carries with it the most poignant sufferings. And not only that, but with and on account of man the whole creation was made subject to vanity and to the bondage of corruption. Berkhof, *Systematic Theology,* 259–60. It is certainly true that when God brings pain and suffering upon people, he has a good purpose. . . . Paul says that "in all things God works for the good of those who love him" (Rom. 8:28). Recognizing and affirming this principle is an essential element in any Christian response to the problem of evil. It is essential to realize that even though God does bring evil into the world, he does it for a good reason. Frame, *The Doctrine of God,* 170.	This recurring wrenching struggle [wherein God allows human suffering] has given rise to a series of standing biblical riddles concerning providence. . . . These remain riddles, not because of the weakness of faith, but precisely because of the tenacity of faith in providence, inasmuch as they affirm the mysterious purpose of God even among the wretched byways and curious meanderings and sufferings and inconveniences of actual lived history. Given the inveterate tendency of human freedom to fall, God continues to come up with merciful alternatives. . . . God is willing to relate responsively to the intrinsically unpredictable development of human freedom. Oden, *The Living God,* 306.	. . . We believe that God *could* have ensured that this world contained no gratuitous evil by refraining from granting other entities significant freedom. . . . We believe that God may at times allow the occurrence of an evil state of affairs in order to bring about some greater good. But we believe that God has chosen to create a world in which individuals possess significant freedom, and hence that God does not as a general rule unilaterally intervene in earthly affairs. And we, like process theists, maintain that humanity not only can, but often does, choose less than the best option available. Thus we, like process theists, believe that much of the pain and suffering we encounter may well be gratuitous—may well not lead to any greater good. Basinger, "Practical Implications"; in Pinnock, *The Openness of God,* 169–70.	. . . Our sufferings also may be conceived as of a piece with a reality which is through-and-through temporal and social. They are the partly avoidable, partly unavoidable, products of finite-free choices and, like everything else, are redolent of eternal significance. Because they, too, occur only within the horizon of God's all-encompassing sympathy, they are the very opposite of the merely indifferent. When they can be prevented, the responsibility for their prevention may now be realized in all its infinite importance; and, when they must be borne with, even that may be understood to have the consolation which alone enables any of us to bear them. Ogden, *The Reality of God,* 64–65.

Open Theism Compared with Other Theological Systems

Related Theological Issues

	Calvinism	Arminianism	Open Theism	Process Theism
Prayer	To prayer, then, are we indebted for penetrating to those riches which are treasured up for us with our heavenly Father. For there is a kind of intercourse between God and men, by which, having entered the upper sanctuary, they appear before Him and appeal to his promises, that when necessity requires they may learn by experiences that what they believed merely on the authority of his word was not in vain. Accordingly, we see that nothing is set before us as an object of expectation from the Lord which we are not enjoined to ask of Him in prayer, so true it is that prayer digs up those treasures which the Gospel of our Lord discovers to the eye of faith. The necessity and utility of this exercise of prayer no words can sufficiently express. Assuredly it is not without cause our heavenly Father declares that our only safety is in calling upon his name, since by it we invoke the presence of his providence to watch over our interests, of his power to sustain us when weak and almost fainting, of his goodness to receive us into favor. Calvin, *Institutes,* 3.20.1.	It is probable, many, perhaps the generality of men . . . are apt to imagine [the portion of the Lord's Prayer that reads "Thy will be done in earth, as it is in heaven"] are only an expression of, or petition for, resignation; for a readiness to suffer the will of God, whatsoever it be, concerning us. . . . But this is not what we pray for in this petition. . . . We pray, not so much for a passive, as for an active conformity to the will of God, in saying, "Thy will be done in earth, as it is in heaven.". . . In other words, we pray that we and all mankind may do the whole will of God in all things . . . in the manner that pleases Him: and, lastly, that we may do it *because* it is His will; that this may be the sole reason and ground, the whole and only motive, of whatsoever we think, or whatsoever we speak or do. Wesley, "Sermon XXI: Upon Our Lord's Sermon on the Mount," VI.III. 9–10; in Sugden, *John Wesley's Fifty-Three Sermons.*	The situation regarding impetratory prayer is quite different in the risk model, which asserts that God enters into genuine personal relations with us. According to the fellowship model God is genuinely responsive to us. . . . Our prayers make a difference to God because of the personal relationship God enters into with us. God chooses to make himself dependent on us for certain things. Sanders, *The God Who Risks,* 271. . . . While much of the trinitarian warfare worldview can be embraced without accepting that the future is to some degree open, accepting the partial openness of the future is particularly advantageous when it comes to making sense of the power and urgency of prayer. If everything is eternally settled ahead of time either in the will or the mind of God, as the blueprint model of providence holds, then it is difficult to explain the urgency and efficacy that Scripture attributes to prayer. Boyd, *Satan and the Problem of Evil,* 230.	Thus one should even ask, for example, whether the new theism enables us so to conceive God that we may meaningfully pray to him as Scripture plainly enjoins us to do. Of course, those who regard this as *the* test question often betray an understanding of prayer that is not only superstitious from the standpoint of secularity, but also sub-Christian by the criterion of faith itself. . . . Whatever else Christian prayers are, they can never be a matter either of informing God as to what he otherwise would not know or of importuning him to do what, but for our prayers, he is unwilling to do. Ogden, *The Reality of God,* 67 n. 105.

Open Theism Compared with Other Theological Systems

Related Theological Issues

	Calvinism	Arminianism	Open Theism	Process Theism
Prayer	Another objection often raised against specific sovereignty centers on . . . petitionary prayer. . . . Petitionary prayer . . . seems useless. After all, if God has already decided what will happen and if his will is immutable, our prayers cannot change anything. We kid ourselves if we think our prayers matter. However, Scripture commands us to pray, and teaches that it makes a difference when we pray. God is depicted as being moved to act, sometimes even to do things he apparently wasn't planning to do. . . . Whatever God does, he can do apart from our prayers. But God decrees means to ends, and he may have ordained that in answer to our prayers he will do a particular work in our life. Perhaps not, but we don't know that either, so we need to pray. It is foolish not to communicate with your creator and God, but God may also have ordained that he would be moved to act as a result of our prayer. Feinberg, *No One Like Him,* 702–3.	God's care of humanity is made known through answering prayers. When Manasseh "in his distress" prayed to the Lord, "God accepted his petition and heard his supplication" (2 Chron. 33:13). Jesus urged his disciples, "Ask, and you will receive" (Matt. 7:7). Oden, *The Living God,* 293. Prayer is a duty which is obligatory upon all men as an expression of the creature's dependence upon the Creator. It may be said that what the habitual sense of reverence is to adoration and praise, the spirit of dependence is to prayer. Wiley, *Christian Theology,* 3.IV.XXX.	God makes himself available to his people. In being available, God provides access that people may call on him. . . . Because God desires a genuine relationship, he is open to his creatures, especially through prayer. . . . Sanders, *The God Who Risks,* 53–54. . . . [Open theists] agree that it is . . . quite reasonable to view petitionary prayer as a means whereby we grant God the permission to influence our noncognitive states of mind and/or share with us those cognitive insights concerning ourselves and others that will help us better live out our Christian commitment in this world. Basinger, "Practical Implications"; in Pinnock, *The Openness of God,* 162. . . . Despite all the pious talk about how God wants and even needs us to pray, many Christians have an understanding of divine sovereignty in which the urgency of prayer simply doesn't make much sense. Regardless of what Scripture teaches . . . they believe that God's plans cannot *truly* be changed; the future is exhaustively settled. . . . What *real* difference could prayer possibly make? Boyd, *God of the Possible,* 95.	Certainly it is meaningless to ask what we could do if God did not help us. He always does help us. The question means, I presume, does God help some more than others, help more sometimes than at other times, or in this way rather than in that way. Hartshorne, *The Divine Relativity,* 146.

Related Theological Issues

	Calvinism	Arminianism	Open Theism	Process Theism
Salvation	The things which have been observed, do also take off the main objections of Arminians against the doctrine of *efficacious grace*; and at the same time, prove the grace of God in a sinner's conversion . . . to be efficacious, yea, and *irresistible* too, if by irresistible is meant, that which is attended with a moral necessity, which it is impossible should ever be violated by any resistance. Edwards, *The Works of Jonathan Edwards: The Freedom of the Will,* 433. . . . The doctrine of monergistic regeneration—or as it was phrased by the older theologians, of "irresistible grace" or "effectual calling"—is the hinge of the Calvinistic soteriology, and lies much more deeply embedded in the system then the doctrine of predestination itself which is popularly looked upon as its hall-mark. Indeed, the soteriological significance of predestination to the Calvinist consists in the safeguard it affords to monergistic regeneration—to purely supernatural salvation. Warfield, *Calvin and Calvinism,* 359.	There is no more fundamental principle [than that of volitional freedom]. It occupies much the same position in this system that the divine sovereignty occupies in Calvinism. As this sovereignty underlies the predestination, the monergism, the irresistibility of grace, and the final perseverance in the one; so freedom underlies the synergism, the real conditionality of salvation, and the possibility of apostasy in the other. In Arminianism freedom must include the power of choosing the good, as the necessary ground of a responsible probation. Repentance and faith as requisite to salvation must be possible; punishable deeds must be avoidable; responsible duties must be practicable. This is the meaning of Arminianism in the maintenance of a universal grace through a universal atonement; a grace which lifts up mankind into freedom, with power to choose the good. Miley, *Systematic Theology,* 1:522.	*Is faith a work?* Scripture seems to confirm this perspective. Throughout both the Old and New Testaments we find the Lord pleading with people to *make a choice* to accept his offer of salvation. . . . It is ultimately up to people as morally responsible agents to choose to accept or reject God's offer of salvation. Boyd, *Satan and the Problem of Evil,* 81. Christians have usually believed that because we are slaves to sin and to Satan . . . we could never choose to accept God's offer of salvation unless God graciously enabled us to do so. Does this view not conflict with the idea that we are self-determining agents in the process of salvation? I do not believe that it does. . . . I, along with other Arminians, deny that the Father draws us and the Spirit enables us *in an irresistible manner*. God graciously makes it *possible* for us to believe. But he does not make it *necessary* for us to believe. Boyd, *Satan and the Problem of Evil,* 82–83.	We should be willing to be damned for the glory of God, but should know that in the very act of so willing, we should, for that moment, enjoy essential salvation. But only for the moment? Yes, and no. We must remember that the divine omniscience overcomes the seeming fragility of achievement and renders it immortal. Thus each moment of true salvation is a thing of beauty and a joy forever in the divine life. In Whitehead's sublime words such moments "perish, and yet live forevermore." Hartshorne, *The Divine Relativity,* 133–34.

Open Theism Compared with Other Theological Systems

Related Theological Issues

	Calvinism	Arminianism	Open Theism	Process Theism
Salvation	What lies at the heart of [Calvin's] soteriology is the absolute exclusion of the creaturely element in the initiation of the saving process, that so the pure grace of God may be magnified. Only so could he express his sense of man's complete dependence as sinner on the free mercy of a saving God; or extrude the evil leaven of Synergism (q.v.) by which. . . . God is robbed of His glory and man is encouraged to think that he owes to some power, some act of choice, some initiative of his own, his participation in that salvation which is in reality all of grace. There is accordingly nothing against which Calvinism sets its face with more firmness than every form and degree of autosoterism. . . . Sinful man stands in need not of inducements or assistance to save himself, but of actual saving; and Jesus Christ has come not to advise, or urge, or induce, or aid him to save himself, but to save him. This is the root of Calvinistic soteriology. . . . Warfield, *Calvin and Calvinism*, 359-60. *Justification is a judicial act of God, in which He declares, on the basis of the righteousness of Jesus Christ, that all the claims of the law are satisfied with respect to the sinner.* It is . . . a declaration respecting the sinner, and not an act or process of renewal, such as regeneration, conversion, and sanctification. Berkhof, *Systematic Theology,* 513.	That predestination is the decree of the good pleasure of God, in Christ, by which he determined, within himself, from all eternity, to justify believers, to adopt them, and to endow them with eternal life, "to the praise of the glory of his grace," and even for the declaration of his justice. This predestination is evangelical, and, therefore, peremptory and irrevocable; and, as the gospel is purely gracious, this predestination is also gracious, according to the benevolent inclination of God in Christ. But that grace excludes every cause which can possibly be imagined to be capable of having proceeded from man, and by which God may be moved to make this decree. Arminius, *Private Disputations,* XL.II.III.	We are even able to hurt God by refusing his offer and by working at cross-purposes to him. Affected by this, God may show anger but mostly sets about restoring the relationship and rebuilding the trust. Pinnock, *Most Moved Mover,* 46. The process of salvation in the divine-human encounter is personal in nature. Because of this, divine risk is not eliminated, since it is possible for us (however unreasonably) to refuse the gift. Even those enabled by God's grace may refuse salvific love; there are no guarantees here. The divine love is patient and enduring, bears with our sinful obduracy and hopes for our return but does not force itself on us. . . . Sanders, *The God Who Risks,* 246.	The presence of God in us is divine grace. It gives rise to adventure, and to art. To it we owe the beauty we experience as well as the discord that makes us restless with the law. It works at all times in all people. The supreme gift is Peace, which is an alignment of ourselves with God's grace. This alignment occurs only through our free decision to live from grace. Cobb, *Process Theology,* 126–27.

Open Theism Compared with Other Theological Systems

Related Theological Issues

	Calvinism	Arminianism	Open Theism	Process Theism
Salvation	The doctrine of the perseverance of the saints is to the effect that they whom God has regenerated and effectually called to a state of grace, can neither totally nor finally fall away from that state, but shall certainly persevere therein to the end to be eternally saved. . . . The doctrine is not merely to the effect that the elect will certainly be saved in the end . . . but teaches very specifically that they who have once been regenerated and effectually called by God to a state of grace, can never completely fall from that state and thus fail to attain eternal salvation, though they may sometimes be overcome by evil and fall into sin. . . . It is, strictly speaking, not man but God who perseveres. Perseverance may be defined as that continuous operation of the Holy Spirit in the believer, by which the work of divine grace that is begun in the heart, is continued and brought to completion. It is because God never forsakes His work that believers continue to stand to the very end. Berkhof, *Systematic Theology,* 545–46.	. . . Those who are branches of Christ, the true vine, may yet finally fall from grace. . . . Those who so effectually know Christ, as by that knowledge to have escaped the pollutions of the world, may yet fall back into those pollutions and perish everlastingly. Wesley, "Predestination Calmly Considered," LXXII–LXXIII; in Outler, *A Library of Protestant Thought: John Wesley.* . . . The atonement of satisfaction, in the Calvinistic sense of it, cannot be true. If the atonement is really for all, and in the same sense sufficient for all, then it must be only provisory, and its saving benefits really conditional. . . . *The vicarious sufferings of Christ are an atonement for sin as a conditional substitute for penalty, fulfilling, on the forgiveness of sin, the obligation of justice and the office of penalty in moral government.* Miley, *Systematic Theology,* 2:68.	Security is linked to our faith-union with Christ. The relationship must be maintained and not be forsaken. . . . The continuation of salvation depends, in part, on the human partner because the relationship is personal and reciprocal. . . . I cannot pretend that the open view of God is very appealing at this point. It may make sense of the biblical exhortations and it may follow from a personal model of salvation but it does not appeal to our self-interest. From a biblical and theological point of view, eternal security is the first petal of Calvinism's TULIP that should fall. . . . It may even be that in heaven there will be no possibility of falling away. The element of risk may belong to the time of our earthly probation. . . . Pinnock, *Most Moved Mover,* 170–71.	

Related Theological Issues

	Calvinism	Arminianism	Open Theism	Process Theism
Salvation	As Scripture, then, clearly shows, we say that God once established by his eternal and unchangeable plan those whom he long before determined once for all to receive into salvation, and those whom, on the other hand, he would devote to destruction. We assert that, with respect to the elect, this plan was founded upon his freely given mercy, without regard to human worth; but by his just and irreprehensible but incomprehensible judgment he has barred the door of life to those whom he has given over to damnation. Now among the elect we regard the call as a testimony of election. Then we hold justification another sign of its manifestation, until they come into the glory in which the fulfillment of that election lies. But as the Lord seals his elect by call and justification, so, by shutting off the reprobate from knowledge of his name or from the sanctification of his Spirit, he, as it were, reveals by these marks what sort of judgment awaits them. Here I shall pass over many fictions that stupid men have invented to overthrow predestination. They need no refutation, for as soon as they are brought forth they abundantly prove their own falsity. I shall pause only over those which either are being argued by the learned or may raise difficulty for the simple, or which impiety speciously sets forth in order to assail God's righteousness. Calvin, *Institutes,* 3.21, conclusion.	We place the form of this predestination in the internal act itself of God, who foreordains to believers this union with Christ their Head, and a participation in his benefits. But we place the end in "the praise of the glory of the grace of God"; and as this grace is the cause of that decree, it is equitable that it should be celebrated by glory, though God, by using it, has rendered it illustrious and glorious. In this place, too, occurs the mention of justice itself, as that by the intervention of which Christ was given as mediator, and faith in him was required; because, without this mediator, God has neither willed to shew mercy, nor to save men without faith in him. But, as this decree of predestination is according to election, which necessarily includes reprobation, we must likewise advert to it. As opposed to election, therefore, we define reprobation to be the decree of God's anger or of his severe will, by which, from all eternity, he determined to condemn to eternal death all unbelievers and impenitent persons, for the declaration of his power and anger; yet so, that unbelievers are visited with this punishment, not only on account of unbelief, but likewise on account of other sins from which they might have been delivered through faith in Christ. Arminius, *Private Disputations,* XL.VI–VII.	In the same way that God predestined and foreknew the death of Jesus without predestining or foreknowing which individuals would condemn him, so God predestined and foreknew the church without predestining or foreknowing which specific individuals would belong to it. . . . When Paul says that God "chose us in Christ before the foundation of the world," he immediately specifies that this predestination was for us "to be holy and blameless before him in love." . . . Note, Paul does *not* say that we were *individually* predestined to be "in Christ." . . . Boyd, *God of the Possible,* 46. Before creation it was possible that no single human would ever come to reciprocate the divine love, but this has not happened. God has achieved his desire with a good number of people. . . . If one of God's plans fails, he has others ready at hand and finds other ways of accomplishing his objectives. Sanders, *The God Who Risks,* 234.	

Open Theism Compared with Other Theological Systems

Related Theological Issues

	Calvinism	Arminianism	Open Theism	Process Theism
Salvation	. . . Hence will necessarily follow the doctrine of particular, eternal, absolute election. For if. . . . God thus makes some saints, and not others, on design or purpose . . . it follows, that God thus distinguished from others, all that ever became true saints, by his eternal design or decree. Edwards, *The Works of Jonathan Edwards: The Freedom of the Will,* 435. [God's] predestination may be defined to be His purpose concerning the everlasting destiny of His rational creatures. His election is His purpose of saving eternally some men and angels . . . this predetermination of men's privileges and destinies by God includes the reprobation of the wicked, as well as the election of the saints. . . . Dabney, *Lectures in Systematic Theology,* XXI:223–24.	. . . We place Christ as the foundation of this predestination, and as the meritorious cause of those blessings which have been destined to believers by that decree. For the love with which God loves men absolutely to salvation, and according to which he absolutely intends to bestow on them eternal life, this love has no existence except in Jesus Christ, the Son of his love, who, both by his efficacious communication, and by his most worthy merits, is the cause of salvation, and not only the dispenser of recovered salvation, but likewise the solicitor, obtainer, and restorer of that salvation which was lost. Therefore, sufficient is not attributed to Christ, when he is called executor of the decree which had been previously made, and without the consideration of him as [the person] on whom that decree is founded. Arminius, *Private Disputations,* XL.IV.	. . . The concept of calling does not imply that God directly decides the eternal destiny of each human being. In fact, we misunderstand the biblical notion of calling, or election, if we think it applies either primarily to individuals or primarily to ultimate human destiny. Throughout the Bible divine election typically represents a corporate call to service. It applies to groups rather than to individuals. . . . Rice, "Biblical Support for a New Perspective"; in Pinnock, *The Openness of God,* 56. . . . The central point of predestination is the goals God sets for his people as a whole, "not the selection of who will become his people." And when God's call does focus on specific individuals, it represents a summons to service, not a guarantee of personal salvation. Rice, "Biblical Support for a New Perspective"; in Pinnock, *The Openness of God,* 57.	

Related Theological Issues

	Calvinism	Arminianism	Open Theism	Process Theism
Salvation	. . . The atonement was intended to propitiate God and to reconcile Him to the sinner. This is undoubtedly the primary idea. . . . It represents the main difference between those who accept the satisfaction doctrine of the atonement and all those who prefer some other theory. Berkhof, *Systematic Theology*, 373. The blood of the sacrifice is interposed between God and the sinner, and in view of it the wrath of God is turned aside. It has the effect, therefore, of warding off the wrath of God from the sinner. Berkhof, *Systematic Theology,* 374. The Bible certainly teaches that the sufferings and death of Christ were vicarious, and vicarious in the strict sense of the word that He took the place of sinners, and that their guilt was imputed, and their punishment transferred, to Him. Berkhof, *Systematic Theology,* 376. It is perfectly true that, according to the penal substitutionary doctrine of the atonement Christ suffered as "the righteous for the unrighteous." . . . Berkhof, *Systematic Theology,* 378.	The teaching of the scripture on this subject may be summed up as follows: The finished work, as accomplished by the Mediator himself, in His relation to mankind, is His divine-human obedience regarded as an expiatory sacrifice: the atonement proper. Then it may be studied in its results to God, as to God and man, and as to man. *First,* it is the supreme manifestation of the glory and consistency of the divine attributes; and, as to this, is termed the righteousness of God. *Second,* as it respects God and man, it is the reconciliation, a word which involves two truths, or rather one truth under two aspects: the propitiation of the divine displeasure against the world is declared; and therefore the sin of the world is no longer a bar to acceptance. *Third,* in its influence on man, it may be viewed as redemption: universal as to the race, limited in its process and consummation to those who believe. Pope, *A Compendium of Christian Theology,* 2:263.	. . . The tendency of the Western church has been to focus almost all its attention on the anthropological dimension of the atonement, usually to the neglect of the cosmic dimension that is central to the New Testament. In the standard Protestant view, the chief thing God was accomplishing when he had Jesus die on the cross was satisfying his perfect justice and thereby atoning for our sins. . . . I maintain, the anthropological significance of Christ's death and resurrection is rooted in something more fundamental and broad that God was aiming at: to defeat once and for all his cosmic archenemy, Satan, along with the other evil powers under his dominion, and thereby to establish Christ as the legitimate ruler of the cosmos. . . . Boyd, *God at War,* 240–41. . . . Atonement is not something an angry God demands, but something a loving God provides. Rice, *The Reign of God,* 177.	

Related Theological Issues

	Calvinism	Arminianism	Open Theism	Process Theism
Salvation	. . . However Christ in some sense may be said to *die for all,* and to redeem all visible Christians, yea, the whole world by his death; yet there must be something *particular* in the design of his death, with respect to such as he intended should actually be saved thereby. . . . God has the actual salvation or redemption of a certain number in his proper absolute design, and of a certain number only. . . . Edwards, *The Works of Jonathan Edwards: The Freedom of the Will,* 435. . . . The atonement, having been worked out by God Himself, is His own personal property and . . . He is absolutely sovereign in the disposal which He chooses to make of it. . . . As relates to the extent of the atonement, the doctrine of the foreknowledge of God is in itself sufficient to prove that in the plan of God Christ died only for those who are actually saved. Boettner, *Studies in Theology,* 316.	The atonement is also grounded in a governmental necessity. God as the infinite moral Being, is characterized by the absolute and essential principles of the true, the right, the perfect and the good. These cannot be abrogated, altered or set aside. He has created a race of beings endowed with the same principles of rational intuition. Moral law, therefore, becomes imperative, and moral government a necessity. As moral Governor, God cannot dispense with the sanctions of those eternal and immutable laws under which alone, His creatures can exist. To repeal the sanctions would be to break down the distinctions between right and wrong, give license to sin, and introduce chaos into a world of order and beauty. God cannot, therefore, set aside the execution of the penalty. He must either inflict retributive justice upon the sinner himself, or maintain public justice by providing a substitute. The governmental theory of the atonement, therefore, makes prominent the sacrifice of Christ as a substitute for penalty. Wiley, *Christian Theology,* 2.III.XXIV.	. . . Many Christian scholars now perceive the suffering of Calvary not as something Jesus offers to God on human behalf, still less as something God inflicts on Jesus (instead of on other human beings), but as the activity of God himself. Rice, "Biblical Support for a New Perspective"; in Pinnock, *The Openness of God,* 45. God takes a risk in creating the sort of world in which he desires a relationship of love but love cannot be forced. This relational, or fellowship, model produces an understanding of sin, election, grace and salvation that is quite different from the manipulative model. Sanders, *The God Who Risks,* 243.	

PART SEVEN
Bibliography

Bibliography

Alexander of Alexandria. *Epistles on the Arian Heresy*, in *The Ante-Nicene Fathers,* Vol. 6, edited by Alexander Roberts and James Donaldson. 1887. Reprint, Grand Rapids: Eerdmans, 1951. Hereafter cited as ANF.

Anselm of Canterbury. *St. Anselm: Basic Writings*. Translated by S. N. Deane. La Salle, Ill: Open Court Publishing Company, 1962.

_________. *Trinity, Incarnation, and Redemption: Three Philosophical Dialogues*. Edited and translated by Jasper Hopkins & Herbert W. Richardson. New York: Harper & Row, 1970.

_________. *Truth, Freedom, and Evil: Three Philosophical Dialogues.* Edited and translated by Jasper Hopkins & Herbert Richardson. New York: Harper & Row, 1967.

Aristides, *Apology.* (ANF, Volume 10).

Arminius, James. *The Works of James Arminius*. Vol. 2. The London Edition, translated by James & William Nicholes. 1875. Reprint, Grand Rapids: Baker, 1999.

_________. *The Works of James Arminius,* 3 vols. Translated by James Nichols and W. R. Bagnall. Buffalo: Derby, Miller, and Orton, 1853.

Arnobius. *The Seven Books of Arnobius* (ANF, Volume 6).

Athenagoras. *A Plea for the Christians* (ANF, Volume 2).

Augustine of Hippo. *Basic Writings of Saint Augustine.* Vol. 2. Edited by Whitney J. Oates. New York: Random House, 1948.

_________. *The City of God.* Translated by Marcus Dods. 1950. Reprint, New York: Modern Library, 1983.

_________. *On Patience*, Electronic version copyright © 1996 by New Advent, Inc. [found at: http://www.newadvent.org/fathers/1315.htm]

_________. *The Works of Saint Augustine: A Translation for the 21st Century.* Translated by Roland Teske, edited by John E. Rotelle. Hyde Park, N.Y.: New City Press, 2001. [Part II Volume 1 & Part III Volume 16 cited]

Basinger, David. *The Case for Freewill Theism: A Philosophical Assessment.* Downers Grove, Ill.: InterVarsity, 1996.

_________. *Divine Power in Process Theism: A Philosophical Critique.* Albany, N.Y.: State University of New York Press, 1988.

Bavinck, Herman. *The Doctrine of God.* Grand Rapids: Eerdmans, 1955.

Baxter, Richard. *The Practical Works of Richard Baxter.* Vol. 3. Morgan, Pa.: Soli Deo Gloria, 2000.

Berkhof, Louis. *Systematic Theology*. Rev. and enl. Grand Rapids: Eerdmans, 1953.

Bernard of Clairvoux. *On Loving God.* Kalamazoo, Mich.: Cistercian, 1973 translation.

Beza, Theodore. *A Little Book of Christian Questions and Responses: In which the Principal Headings of the Christian Religion are Briefly Set Forth.* 1570. Reprint, Allison Park, Pa.: Pickwick Publications, 1986.

Boethius. *Consolation of Philosophy.* Translated by Joel C. Relihan. Indianapolis: Hackett, 2001.

Boettner, Loraine. *Studies in Theology.* Phillipsburg, N. J.: Presbyterian & Reformed, 1978.

Boston, Thomas. "Properties of God's Decrees Explained," in *The Beauties of Boston: A Selection of His Writings*. Inverness, Scotland: Christian Focus, 1979.

Boyd, Gregory A. *God at War: The Bible and Spiritual Conflict.* Downers Grove, Ill.: InterVarsity, 1997.

_________. *God of the Possible: Does God Ever Change His Mind?* Grand Rapids: Baker, 2000.

_________. *Satan and the Problem of Evil: Constructing a Trinitarian Warfare Theodicy.* Downers Grove, Ill: InterVarsity, 2001.

Brown, Delwin, Ralph E. James, Jr., & Gene Reeves, eds. *Process Philosophy and Christian Thought.* Indianapolis: Bobbs-Merrill, 1971.

Bucer, Martin. *Common Places of Martin Bucer.* Translated and edited by D. F. Wright. Appleford, England: Sutton Courtenay, 1972.

Burtner, Robert W. & Robert E. Chiles, eds. *A Compend of Wesley's Theology.* Nashville: Abingdon, 1954.

Buswell, James Oliver. *A Systematic Theology of the Christian Religion.* Vol. 1 (Grand Rapids: Zondervan, 1962.

Bibliography

Calvin, John. *The Institutes of the Christian Religion,* 2 volumes. Beveridge translation. 1845. Reprint, Grand Rapids: Eerdmans, 1975.

__________. The Institutes of the Christian Religion, 2 volumes. Translated by Ford Lewis Battles. Philadelphia: Westminster, 1960.

Cannon, William Ragsdale.

The Theology of John Wesley. Nashville: Abingdon-Cokesbury, 1946.

Carter, Charles W., ed. *A Contemporary Wesleyan Theology: Biblical, Systematic, and Practical.* Grand Rapids: Francis Asbury, 1983.

Chafer, Lewis Sperry. *Systematic Theology.* Vol. 1. Dallas: Dallas Seminary Press, 1947.

Charnock, Stephen, *The Existence and Attributes of God.* 1682. Reprint, Grand Rapids: Baker, 1996.

Clement of Alexandria. *Stromata* (ANF, Volume 2).

Clement of Rome. *Epistle to the Corinthians* (ANF, Volume 1).

Cobb, John B., Jr. *Christian Natural Theology.* Philadelphia: Westminster, 1965.

__________. *God and the World.* Philadelphia: Westminster, 1965.

__________. *Reenchantment Without Supernaturalism: A Process Philosophy of Religion.* Ithaca, N.Y.: Cornell University Press, 2000.

__________. "Christian Natural Theology," in *Process Philosophy and Christian Thought,* edited by Delwin Brown, Ralph E. James, Jr., & Gene Reeves. Indianapolis: Bobbs-Merrill, 1971.

__________. "A Whiteheadian Christology," in *Process Philosophy and Christian Thought,* edited by Delwin Brown, Ralph E. James, Jr., & Gene Reeves. Indianapolis: Bobbs-Merrill, 1971.

__________. "A Whiteheadian Doctrine of God," in *Process Philosophy and Christian Thought,* edited by Delwin Brown, Ralph E. James, Jr., & Gene Reeves. Indianapolis: Bobbs-Merrill, 1971.

Cobb, John B., Jr. and David Ray Griffin, *Process Theology: An Introductory Exposition.* Philadelphia: Westminster, 1976.

Cobb, John B. and Clark H. Pinnock, eds. *Searching for an Adequate God: A Dialogue between Process and Free Will Theists.* Grand Rapids: Eerdmans, 2000.

Cyprian. *Epistle to the People of Thibaris* (ANF, Volume 5).

__________. *The Treatises of Cyprian* (ANF, Volume 5).

Cyril of Alexandria. *Ad Calosyrius.* In *Saint Cyril of Alexandria: Letters 51–110,* translated by John I. McEnerney. Washington, D.C.: Catholic University of America Press, 1987.

Cyril of Jerusalem. *Catechetical Lectures* in *The Nicene and Post-Nicene Fathers,* Series II, Vol. 7, edited by Philip Schaff and Henry Wace. Edinburgh: T&T Clark, 1885 translation. Hereafter cited as NPNF.

Dabney, Robert L. *Lectures in Systematic Theology.* 1871. Reprint, Grand Rapids: Zondervan, 1972.

Davis, Stephen T. *Logic and the Nature of God.* Grand Rapids: Eerdmans, 1983.

Dionysius the Great. *On John* (ANF, Volume 6).

Dombrowski, Daniel A. *Analytic Theism, Hartshorne, and the Concept of God.* Albany, N.Y.: State University of New York Press, 1996.

Edwards, Jonathan. *The Works of Jonathan Edwards: Freedom of the Will.* Edited by Paul Ramsey. New Haven, Conn.: Yale University Press, 1957.

__________. *The Works of Jonathan Edwards: The "Miscellanies" 501–832.* Edited by Ava Chamberlain. New Haven, Conn.: Yale University Press, 2000.

__________. *The Works of Jonathan Edwards: The "Miscellanies" 833–1152.* Edited by Amy Plantinga Pauw. New Haven, Conn.: Yale University Press, 2002.

__________. *The Works of Jonathan Edwards: Writings on the Trinity, Grace, and Faith.* Edited by Sang Hyun Lee. New Haven, Conn.: Yale University Press, 2003.

Erickson, Millard J. *Christian Theology.* Grand Rapids: Baker, 1985.

Feinberg, John S. *No One Like Him: The Doctrine of God.* Wheaton, Ill.: Crossway, 2001.

Flavel, John, *The Works of John Flavel.* Vol. 4. Reprint, Carlisle, Pa.: Banner of Truth Trust, 1982

Bibliography

Frame, John M. *The Doctrine of God: A Theology of Lordship*. Phillipsburg, N. J.: Presbyterian & Reformed Publishing, 2002.

__________. *No Other God: A Response to Open Theism*. Phillipsburg, N.J.: Presbyterian & Reformed Publishing, 2001.

Geach, Peter T. *Providence and Evil*. London: Cambridge University Press, 1977.

Geisler, Norman. *Creating God in the Image of Man?: Neotheism's Dangerous Drift*. Minneapolis: Bethany House, 1997.

Geisler, Norman L. & H. Wayne House. *The Battle for God: Responding to the Challenge of NeoTheism*. Grand Rapids: Kregel, 2001.

Gill, John. *The Cause of God and Truth*. London: W. H. Collingridge, 1885.

Goodwin, Thomas. *The Works of Thomas Goodwin*. Vol. 10. 1861. Reprint, Eureka, Calif.: Tanski, 1996.

Gregory of Nyssa. *Against Eunomius* (NPNF, Series II, Volume 5)

Gregory Thaumaturgus, *Metaphrase of the Book of Ecclesiastes* (ANF, Volume 6)

__________. *Twelve Topics on the Faith* (ANF, Volume 6).

Griffin, David Ray. *God, Power, and Evil: A Process Theodicy*. Philadelphia: Westminster, 1976.

__________. "Process Theology and the Christian Good News: A Response to Classical Free Will Theism," in *Searching for an Adequate God: A Dialogue between Process and Free Will Theists*, edited by John B. Cobb, Jr. & Clark H. Pinnock. Grand Rapids: Eerdmans, 2000.

__________. "Schubert Ogden's Christology and the Possibilities of Process Philosophy," in *Process Philosophy and Christian Thought*, edited by Delwin Brown, Ralph E. James, Jr., & Gene Reeves. Indianapolis: Bobbs-Merrill, 1971.

Griffin, David Ray and Thomas J. J. Altizer. *John Cobb's Theology in Process*. Philadelphia: Westminster, 1977.

Guthrie, William. *The Christian's Great Interest*. 1658. Reprint, Carlisle, Pa.: Banner of Truth Trust, 1994.

Hamilton, Peter N. "Some Proposals for a Modern Christology," in *Process Philosophy and Christian Thought*, edited by Delwin Brown, Ralph E. James, Jr., & Gene Reeves. Indianapolis: Bobbs-Merrill, 1971.

Hartshorne, Charles. *The Divine Relativity: A Social Conception of God*. New Haven, Conn.: Yale University Press, 1948.

__________. *Omnipotence and Other Theological Mistakes*. Albany, N.Y.: State University of New York Press, 1994.

__________. *A Process Christology*. Lanham, Md.: University Press of America, 1990.

Hasker, William. *God, Time, and Knowledge*. Ithaca, N.Y.: Cornell University Press, 1989.

__________. *Metaphysics: Constructing a World View*. Downers Grove, Ill.: InterVarsity, 1983.

Helm, Paul. *Eternal God: A Study of God without Time*. Oxford: Clarendon, 1988.

Henry, Carl F. H. *God, Revelation and Authority: God Who Speaks and Shows*, Vol. 3, part 2. Waco, Tex: Word Books, 1979.

__________. *God, Revelation and Authority: God Who Speaks and Shows*, Vol. 4, part 3. Waco, Tex.: Word Books, 1979.

__________. *God, Revelation and Authority: God Who Stands and Stays*, Vol. 4, part 1. Waco, Tex.: Word Books, 1982.

Hilary of Poitiers, *On the Trinity* (NPNF, Series II, Volume 9).

Hippolytus, *Against the Heresy of Noetus* (ANF, Volume 5).

__________. *Refutation of All Heresies* (ANF, Volume 5).

Hodge, Archibald Alexander. *Outlines of Theology*. Grand Rapids: Eerdmans, 1949.

Hodge, Charles. *Systematic Theology*. Vol. 1. Grand Rapids: Eerdmans, 1952.

Hooker, Thomas. *Thomas Hooker: Writings in England and Holland, 1626-1633*. Cambridge, Mass.: Harvard University Press, 1975.

Bibliography

Howell, Nancy R. "Openness and Process Theism: Respecting the Integrity of the Two Views," in *Searching for an Adequate God: A Dialogue between Process and Free Will Theists*. Grand Rapids: Eerdmans, 2000.

__________. "In Response to David Wheeler," in *Searching for an Adequate God: A Dialogue between Process and Free Will Theists*. Grand Rapids: Eerdmans, 2000.

Ignatius of Antioch, *Epistle to Polycarp* (ANF, Volume 1).

__________. *To the Ephesians* (ANF, Volume 1).

Irenaeus. *Against Heresies* (ANF, Volume 1).

John Chrysostom. cited in *Catena Aurea* by Thomas Aquinas. Christian Classics Ethereal Library at www.ccel.org/a/aquinas/catena/home.

Justin Martyr. *Dialogue with Trypho* (ANF, Volume 1).

__________. *First Apology* (ANF, Volume 1).

Knox, John, *Works of John Knox,* Vol. 3, edited by David Laing. Edinburgh: J. Thin, 1895.

__________. *Works of John Knox,* Vol. 5, edited by David Laing. Edinburgh: J. Thin, 1895.

Lactantius. *The Divine Institutes* (ANF, Volume 8).

Langford, Thomas A., ed. *Wesleyan Theology: A Sourcebook.* Durham, N.C.: Labyrinth, 1984.

Loomer, Bernard M. "Christian Faith and Process Philosophy," in *Process Philosophy and Christian Thought,* edited by Delwin Brown, Ralph E. James, Jr., & Gene Reeves. Indianapolis: Bobbs-Merrill, 1971.

Luther, Martin. *Martin Luther on the Bondage of the Will: A New Translation.* Edited by J. I. Packer and O. R. Johnston. Westwood, N.J.: Revell, 1957.

__________. *What Luther Says: An Anthology,* 3 volumes. Edited by Ewald M. Plass. Saint Louis: Concordia, 1959.

__________. *Works*, 55 volumes. Edited by Jaroslav Pelikan, St. Louis: Concordia, 1986.

Mathetes. *Epistle to Diognetus* (ANF, Volume 1).

McGregor-Wright, R. K. *No Place for Sovereignty: What's Wrong with FreeWill Theism'*Downers Grove, Ill.: InterVarsity, 1995.

Melanchthon, Philip. *Melanchthon on Christian Doctrine.* New York, N.Y.: Oxford University Press, 1965.

Melito of Sardis. *Remains of the Second and Third Century* (ANF, Volume 8).

Methodius. *Three Fragments on the Passion of Christ* (ANF, Volume 6).

Miley, John. *Systematic Theology*, 2 volumes. New York: Hunt & Eaton, 1892.

Morris, Thomas V. *Divine and Human Action: Essays in the Metaphysics of Theism.* Ithica, N.Y.: Cornell University Press, 1988.

Muller, Richard A. *God, Creation, and Providence in the Thought of Jacob Arminius: Sources and Directions of Scholastic Protestantism in the Era of Early Orthodoxy*. Grand Rapids: Baker, 1991.

Nash, Ronald H. *The Concept of God: An Exploration of Contemporary Difficulties with the Attributes of God.* Grand Rapids: Zondervan, 1983.

Novatian of Rome. *Treatise Concerning the Trinity* (ANF, Volume 5).

Oden. Thomas C. *The Living God.* San Francisco: Harper & Row, 1987.

Ogden, Schubert M. *The Reality of God and Other Essays.* New York: Harper & Row, 1963.

__________. "Toward a New Theism," in *Process Philosophy and Christian Thought,* edited by Delwin Brown, Ralph E. James, Jr., & Gene Reeves. Indianapolis: Bobbs-Merrill, 1971.

Ogletree, Thomas W. "A Christological Assessment of Dipolar Theism," in *Process Philosophy and Christian Thought,* edited by Delwin Brown, Ralph E. James, Jr., & Gene Reeves. Indianapolis: Bobbs-Merrill, 1971.

Origen. *Commentary on the Epistle to the Romans*, cited in *Ancient Christian Commentary* by Thomas C. Oden. Downers Grove, Ill.: InterVarsity, 2000.

__________. *De Principiis* (ANF, Volume 4).

Outler, Albert C., ed. *A Library of Protestant Thought: John Wesley*. New York: Oxford University Press, 1964.

Bibliography

Owen, John. *The Works of John Owen.* 23 Volumes. Edited by William H. Goold. Edinburgh: T & T Clark, 1862. [Volumes 1, 2 & 20 cited]

Packer, James I. *Evangelism and the Sovereignty of God.* Downers Grove, Ill.: InterVarsity, 1976.

Pack, James I. "Theism for Our Time," in *God Who Is Rich in Mercy*, by Peter T. O'Brien and David G. Peterson. Grand Rapids: Baker, 1986.

Perkins, William. *The Work of William Perkins.* Edited by Ian Breward. Appleford, England: Sutton Courtenay, 1970.

Pink, Arthur W. *The Attributes of God: A Solemn and Blessed Contemplation of Some of the Wondrous and Lovely Perfections of the Divine Character.* Swengel, Pa.: Reiner Publications, n.d.

Pinnock, Clark. *Most Moved Mover: A Theology of God's Openness.* Grand Rapids: Baker, 2001.

Pinnock, Clark H. ed. *The Grace of God, the Will of Man: A Case for Arminianism.* Grand Rapids: Academie Books, 1989.

__________. *The Openness of God: A Biblical Challenge to the Traditional Understanding of God.* Downers Grove, Ill.: InterVarsity, 1994.

Pittenger, Norman. *God's Way with Men.* Gettysburg, Pa.: Judson, 1969.

Polycarp. *Martyrdom of Polycarp* (ANF, Volume 1).

Pope, William Burt. *A Compendium of Christian Theology: Analytical Outlines of a Course of Theological Study.* Vol. 1. Cincinnati: Walden & Stowe, 1881.

Reeves, Gene & Brown, Delwin. "The Development of Process Theology," in *Process Philosophy and Christian Thought,* edited by Delwin Brown, Ralph E. James, Jr., & Gene Reeves. Indianapolis: Bobbs-Merrill, 1971.

Reymond, Robert L. *A New Systematic Theology of the Christian Faith.* Nashville: Thomas Nelson, 1998.

Rice, Richard. *The Reign of God: An Introduction to Christian Theology from a Seventh-Day Adventist Perspective.* Berrien Springs, Mich.: Andrews University Press, 1985.

Salvian the Presbyter, cited in *The Ancient Christian Commentary on Scripture: Old Testament,* edited by Thomas Oden. Downers Grove, Ill.: InterVarsity, 2001.

Sanders, John. *The God Who Risks: A Theology of Providence.* Downers Grove, Ill.: InterVarsity, 1998.

Shedd, W. G. T. *Dogmatic Theology.* Vol. 1. New York: Scribner's Sons, 1888.

Shepard, Thomas. *The Works of Thomas Shepard.* Vol. 1. 1853. Reprint, New York: AMS, 1967.

Sibbes, Richard. *Works of Richard Sibbes.* Edited by Alexander B. Grosart. 1864. Reprint, Edinburgh: Banner of Truth Trust, 1979.

Strong, Augustus Hopkins. *Systematic Theology: The Doctrine of God.* Philadelphia: American Baptist Publication Society, 1907.

Suchocki, Marjorie Hewitt. *God, Christ, Church: A Practical Guide to Process Theology.* New York: Crossroad, 1991.

Sugden, Edward H., ed. *John Wesley's Fifty-Three Sermons.* Nashville: Abingdon, 1983.

Swinburne, Richard. *The Coherence of Theism.* Oxford: Clarendon, 1977.

Tatian. *Address to the Greeks* (ANF, Volume 2).

Tertullian. *Against Hermogenes* (ANF, Volume 3).

__________. *Against Marcion* (ANF, Volume 3).

__________. *Against Praxeas* (ANF, Volume 3).

__________. *An Exhortation to Chastity* (ANF, Volume 4).

__________. *On Fasting* (ANF, Volume 4).

Theophilus. *Theophilus to Autolycus* (ANF, Volume 2).

Thiessen, Henry Clarence. *Lectures in Systematic Theology.* Grand Rapids: Eerdmans, 1979.

Thomas Aquinas. *An Aquinas Reader.* Rev. ed. Edited by Mary T. Clark. New York: Fordham University Press, 2000.

Bibliography

__________. *Basic Writings of Saint Thomas Aquinas,* Vol. 1, edited by Anton C. Pegis. New York: Random House, 1945.

__________. *Summa contra Gentiles,* 5 volumes. Notre Dame, Ind.: University of Notre Dame Press, 1963. [*Summa of Christian Teaching* is found in the Leone Edition 13–15, 1930]

Turretin, Francis. *Institutes of Elenctic Theology*. Vol. 1. 1685. Reprint, Phillipsburg, N.J.: Presbyterian & Reformed, 1992.

Vos, Geerhardus. *Biblical Theology: Old and New Testaments*. Grand Rapids: Eerdmans, 1948.

Ward, Keith. *Rational Theology and the Creativity of God.* Oxford: Blackwell, 1982.

Ware, Bruce A. *God's Lesser Glory: The Diminished God of Open Theism*. Wheaton, Ill.: Crossway, 2000.

Warfield, Benjamin Breckinridge. *Biblical and Theological Studies.* Edited by Samuel Craig. Philadelphia: Presbyterian & Reformed, 1952.

__________. *Calvin and Calvinism*. New York: Oxford University Press, 1931.

__________. *Limited Inspiration.* Reprint, Grand Rapids: Baker, 1961.

__________. *Selected Shorter Writings of Benjamin B. Warfield I.* Edited by John E. Meeter. Nutley, N.J.: Presbyterian & Reformed, 1970.

Wesley, John. *The Works of John Wesley*, Vol. 6. Grand Rapids: Zondervan, 1872.

Wheeler, David L. "Confessional Communities and Public Worldviews: A Case Study," in *Searching for an Adequate God: A Dialogue between Process and Free Will Theists.* Grand Rapids: Eerdmans, 2000.

Whitehead, Alfred North. *Process and Reality: An Essay in Cosmology.* New York: Macmillan, 1929.

__________. *Religion in the Making.* London: Cambridge University Press, 1927.

Wiley, H. Orton. *Christian Theology,* 3 volumes. Kansas City, Mo.: Beacon Hill, 1940.

Zwingli, Ulrich. *On Providence and Other Essays.* Edited by S. M. Jackson and W. J. White. 1922. Reprint, Durham, N. C.: Labyrinth, 1983.